THE
DIVINE
VISITOR

WHAT REALLY HAPPENED
WHEN GOD CAME DOWN

JACK HAYFORD

INTEGRITY®
PUBLISHERS
Nashville

Produced with the assistance of The Livingstone Corporation (www.LivingstoneCorp.com). Introductions written by Greg Asimakoupoulos.

Cover Design: Brand Navigation, LLC—DeAnna Pierce, Terra Petersen, Bill Chiaravalle | www.brandnavigation.com
Cover Photo: Steve Gardner/PixelWorks Studio
Interior Design: Inside Out Design & Typesetting

ISBN 1-59145-306-2

Printed in the United States of America
05 06 07 08 09 BVG 9 8 7 6 5 4 3 2 1

*To faithful pastor-shepherds everywhere who
so often serve selflessly and sacrificially
as appointed stewards of what the
Great Shepherd—the Divine Visitor—
brought to us!*

Contents

INTRODUCTION

*Q*uite possibly you were among the millions who saw Mel Gibson's *The Passion of the Christ.* His epic movie chronicling the final hours of Jesus' earthly life played to packed-movie houses in the weeks leading up to Easter of 2004. The popularity of the blood-drenched film caught critics by surprise. People of faith, the spiritually curious, and those intrigued by the cultural phenomenon, flocked to see an R-rated movie (due to the explicit violence) with English subtitles. In the year it was released *The Passion* was the third-highest-grossing movie. Ticket sales world-wide were $610 million including more than $370 million in North America. Our fascination with the Lord's suffering didn't end there, however; on the first day *The*

Passion was released on DVD for public purchase, four million copies were sold. It was estimated that DVD sales would ultimately reach the vicinity of 15 million to 18 million copies.

But think with me about Christ's suffering. Does it speak to you of death, or of dynamic? I want to affirm its dynamism, because there is a dynamic in an uncluttered insight into the suffering of Jesus Christ. Religious forms in art and practice tend to reduce any remembrance of Christ's suffering to a maudlin mourning. A pitiful, regret-filled, if not weepy, exercise in pointlessness too often ensues. One would surmise that some goal of godliness was being proposed; that God would be especially delighted if we would all feel worse about the fact that Jesus died as though the quest for spirituality is a contest in contrition.

But would you please, just for a moment, feature yourself in Jesus' place? Do you see Him as self-pitying? Try to imagine Him saying, "I wish you would be more despondent when you think of everything I did for you. You know, it really did hurt a lot."

Such a caricature is a virtual sacrilege. It is certainly unrepresentative of the Christ we see during His lifetime, and even less representative of the Christ we now meet enthroned in the heavens, at the right hand of the Father God on high. We can no more imagine Jesus being pathetic than we can imagine any psychologically healthy person wanting people to "feel bad for Him." No, Jesus isn't pitiful or self-pitying. But it can add to our blessing and wisdom to understand His suffering, because He experienced it all for very real purposes—purposes that can be applied to a practical outworking in our lives today. And I would like to invite you to join me in thinking through Christ's sufferings—His wounds, His blood, and His death. What we saw in Gibson's *The Passion* did not tell the whole story. It left us feeling more sorrowful than celebrative. As we look at the bigger picture found in Scripture, I am hoping we can better capture the meaning of all He came to do for us, and the power He wants to give us through it all today.

There is power here that could never come from a self-inflicted spirit of mourning. It's a power born of the Holy Spirit-anointed perspective that comes when we have insight into how and why Jesus suffered and what His suffering accomplished. With that insight we can learn to receive His provision and participate in it with understanding. So let's do it. Let's pursue that insight. Think with me about the coming of the Visitor.

THE COMING
OF THE VISITOR

1

*A*dam had been in the service three years. Although he'd seen his family periodically while stationed stateside, once he was deployed to Iraq he knew he wouldn't get home for at least a year. When his two weeks of leave finally approached, Adam called his folks alerting them to his plans to come home. He didn't tell them the exact day. He wanted to surprise them. Since his family lived on a small farm one hundred miles from a major city, getting home would require Adam to take a series of buses from the base where the military transport landed. It was in the middle of the night when the Greyhound dropped the uniformed soldier off at the deserted depot in the small Kansas town. The excited but weary soldier started to walk the fifteen miles towards his parents' place. After about an hour of walking, he slid his heavy duffle bag off his shoulder and rested on it on the side of the road. Within a few minutes a car approached. Adam jumped to his feet and waved at the driver to slow down. When asked if he could get a lift a few miles up the road, the driver invited him to hop in.

Just as the pre-dawn sky brightened, Adam was deposited at the long gravel road that led to the old farmhouse. A neighbor's dog barked as the young sergeant bounded up the front steps. Having heard the barking, Adam's little sister woke up and looked out her second-floor bedroom window eying her soldier brother's silhouette.

Running downstairs, she raced into Adam's open arms. He brought the index finger of his right hand over his broad smile. "Shhh." He didn't want to wake his folks prematurely. Filling the coffee maker with water and a filter-full of coffee, he waited for the fresh-brewed smell to permeate the house. Waking to the aroma they were typically responsible for, the middle-age parents clad in bathrobes walked into the kitchen wondering what was going on. The initial screams of surprise were soon replaced with tears of joy. The much-anticipated visitor had finally arrived. A morning cup of coffee had never tasted so good. A mom and a dad felt the incredible relief knowing that their son was finally home. As for Adam, he had the satisfaction of knowing that the surprise he had imagined on that twelve-hour flight across the Atlantic had come off without a hitch.

ISN'T IT WONDERFUL TO RECEIVE A TIMELY VISIT from a welcomed friend or loved one? If you've ever had someone you haven't seen in a long time surprise you, it's easy to imagine what it must have been like for that soldier's family. There are few things as wonderful as a visit from someone we dearly long to see.

There are few things as wonderful as a visit from someone we dearly long to see.

When the visitor is someone we know and care about, even planned visits are happy occasions. It is likely we have also experienced the exact opposite—you know, the awkwardness in the arrival of an unexpected guest when everything is a mess. When we aren't prepared for company, the joy of their arrival can be somewhat diminished. And then, how many of us have known the loneliness and disappointment of having been forgotten, left alone, when no one came to visit at all?

Both the positive and negative remembrances of such experiences heighten our sensitivities as to the significance of having a visitor come. And that's why we begin here, because our focus on this text is that God became a visitor. Let's read Hebrews 2:6–9:

> "What is man that You are mindful of him, Or the son of man that You take care of him? You have made him a little lower than the angels; You have crowned him with glory and honor, And set him over the works of Your hands. You have put all things in subjection under his feet." For in that He put all in subjection under him, He left nothing that is not put under him. But now we do not yet see all things put under him. But we see Jesus, who was made a little lower than the angels, for the suffering of death crowned with glory and honor, that He, by the grace of God, might taste death for everyone.

This reference to the coming of our Visitor, the Savior, draws us back to the King James Version of the Bible that reads:

> What is man, that thou art mindful of him? or the son of man, that thou visitest him?

The phrase in the New King James Version, "that You take care of him," is derived from the poignant Greek verb *episkeptomai. Episkeptomai* refers to the whole idea of a visitor in the fullness of care that comes from a visit, a visitor, or a visitation. The idea is one of caring—caring so much that a person makes the point to come and visit a friend with the tenderness, for example, of a gentle family physician—one who would come to make a house call. Remember those days? That is exactly what we are being told in the Scriptures. The Great Physician has rung your bell, medical bag in hand. God became a Visitor to mankind. And in His coming, we—all of us—experienced a visitation. And like the soldier surprising his parents, God's visit was planned for dramatic effect.

THINK WITH ME ABOUT THIS TENDER TRUTH. FIRST, what was His reason for the visit? That is what the prophet is asking when he says, "What is man that You are mindful of him, Or the son of man that You take care of him?" He is asking, "What is the reason? What could prompt this?"

The following words are taken from Psalm 8 in which David, that ancient songwriter, relates his awe as he observes the midnight sky. Studying the star-spangled beauty he says, "God, when I look at the vastness of space and the marvel of creation around me, I say, 'Why do You even bother with man?' And still, You've crowned him with glory and honor. You've given him dominion over the works of Your hands!" (Psalm 8:3–6, paraphrased).

The Scriptures repeatedly assert man's significance in the divine design amid the cosmic order of things. But too seldom is that noted, for in contrast, to the intent of the text, people often suppose, "What is man?" to somehow assert man's worthlessness, rather than the distinct glory the Bible declares is inherent in God's purpose for us. However needy we are in our human helplessness and sin, God never forgets the worthy purpose He had and has for us. And in grace—unrelenting and unforgetful—He comes to us to visit us with life, health, and recovery.

On the tongue of the unknowing, the question "What is man?" may even span the spectrum of expression from an honest-hearted inquiry of human meaning, to a cynical epithet spat in scorn. One may honestly wonder what man's purposes could be, while another may defiantly denigrate any presumption of purpose. How easily can any of us allow ourselves to be reduced to the supposedly humble and theologically correct proposition that if there is a God, then how arrogant we are to suppose significance for ourselves. The theologian may denounce worth, asserting the fact of our lostness. But a lost diamond, though lost, doesn't reduce in value. It is only separated from its proper place with its owner. The cynic may scorn human significance amidst the sprawling cosmos of an awesome creation, but our smallness doesn't remove meaning any more than a silicon chip's size suggests it is negligible in its content.

Doubters may make us nothing more than an advanced collection of cells in constant chemical transition. Some will say we are but temporary objects destined for survival of the fittest at best, and headed for pointless extinction at worst. In such an atmosphere, a voice shouts, "How dare you propose 'divine intent!' After all, we, whose backaches testify to our animal descent, barely able to stand upright, while occupying an insignificant planet in sprawling space, and twirling around a mediocre star—how presumptuous to claim significance, being nothing more than mere products evolving from mud and slime."

"Best admit," the scoffer insists, "your role is to simply survive on this twisting rock, wandering through a galaxy that is but one among billions, spinning randomly through a measureless cosmos."

But a stark rebuttal to this human doubt and scoffing and sometimes religious pretension at humility appears in our text. Man's worth and destiny are asserted in God's Word. At the heart of God's purpose in providing man's redemption is this lofty truth: He has a cosmic intention in man's creation, and His coming to visit man is key to that intent being realized.

With even more love for His creation than the home-bound soldier had for his family, the Creator attests to the worth of His creation. Our emphasis on the Bible's declaration of a phenomenal destiny for man is not empty ego gratification; it's a simple exercise in honesty before God's Word. And to see this in His Word is to see why He was willing to pay so exorbitant a price to regain mankind, a price that begins with His stooping to earth, condescending to come, and revealing, above all, a love that cared enough to pay a visit.

THE SCENARIO UNFOLDS IN THE BIBLE'S OPENING chapters. Almighty God is forced to deal with a crisis regarding His beloved creature: man. Man has breached a divinely endowed trust. Because of this, he has suffered a loss, which can only be reinstated to the Creator's intended order by His loving initiative. The distance between the exalted God and the broken race of man can only be spanned from Deity's side.

And He does it. He chooses to come. He chooses to care. And it is before this awesome fact that the psalmist marvels, "My God, what a wonder! What must You have in mind for mankind that You should visit him?"

But why a visitor? Visitors come for a variety of reasons. A visitor may come when someone is sick, ill, or infirm. He may visit the victim of an accident—or he may come to assist somehow when help is needed. One visitor may simply come to show friendliness, while another's arrival may be to give comfort when someone has died. Another visitor's presence could signal that someone needs tutoring, and a time has been set for the lesson: "Shall we say once a week at four o'clock, on Thursday afternoon? Fine. Your piano teacher will be there."

A visitor may come simply to make an acquaintance: "Hello there. We noticed you just moved in a few days ago. We live next door and just came over to introduce ourselves and to welcome you."

Visitors from a local church arrive at your front door to acknowledge the fact that you were at last Sunday's worship celebration. They want to thank you for your attendance, answer any questions you might have, and perhaps offer you a small loaf of freshly baked bread before inviting you to return next week.

Visitors come when people are hungry or needy: "We are from the social welfare agency. We have been advised there is need here, and we have provisions available for your family if you'd like them."

Or a visitor may come for simpler, more sentimental reasons. All our hearts are warmed when someone arrives or calls just to say, "I came by today just to tell you I love you."

Ah, we need that—a visit, just because somebody loves and cares for us.

Visitors also come at very painful times. The telephone rings: "You had better come quickly; he's weakening. There isn't much time left, at least in this world." And against apparent hopelessness, the visit is made. Relatives fly in from all points, hoping for one last opportunity to see a loved one.

These are reasons why visits are made, because people care about each other. And considering all of the above reasons can deepen our appreciation for that occasion when our Lord—God Himself—came to visit us. For His coming was in the style of all the aforementioned situations.

Someone had died; a race had lost its living relationship with God. And since the death-plague infected our whole race, all were sick, and He came to visit us in our sickness.

And there was need—hungry people everywhere, then as today. And beyond his immediate need of bread for his body, man's soul still clamors for something to satisfy his deepest hunger. Covetousness goads us. The need to have something breeds an appetite for emptiness. An unending lust for "more" tugs at us all and like the prodigal son, we, too, often end our quest in a pigsty.

Most people who sin do so more from desperation than out of a conscious disobedience.

It is difficult to criticize the sinning that results from this human hunger, the need to have. I have concluded that most people who sin do so more from desperation than out of a conscious disobedience—sinning not so much because of an intended rebellion as because of blind hunger and not knowing where to find Life-Bread. This is why the Visitor came saying, "I have brought the bread; indeed, I am the Bread of Life, the answer to your hunger."

This holy Visitor also came to establish acquaintance: "You can know the Living God, truly know Him personally. I have come to show you the Father."

If ever a teacher came to visit, this is the one. He came to teach us clearly what the Father is like. "If you've seen Me," Jesus said, "you have seen the Father." He says that to those He visits. Both in John's Gospel and Paul's Colossian letter, Jesus is set forth as the precise revelation of Father God's nature. He's at direct contrast to the images which human imagination sometimes projects. How many distorted images of "father" often haunt us, and how many humanly fallible authority figures sour our view of God? But look, shedding His light and dispelling the shadows of confusion, Jesus visits us—visits to show how the eternal Father expresses authority and love in equal balance—and we see the complete reality of God in this Visitor. For in Him—in Christ—dwells all the fullness of the Godhead bodily.

And our Visitor also came just to say, "I love you."

Dear friend, it is perfectly appropriate simply to look into Jesus' face, and let the full measure of His words touch your emotions. He does love you—deeply and thoroughly. And unless we gain a deep sense of that love, we are going to miss more than we can possibly imagine. Let your eyes see Him. See Jesus as He weeps over Jerusalem, saying, "The day of your visitation has come and you didn't recognize it." Let those words of the Visitor and His visitation clarify our need for and our wisdom in firmly grasping and thoroughly understanding this fact: We have been visited. Let those words sink into your soul, dear one, for no matter what you or I face, the Visitor is there, bringing a power that can flow to us now because of the visit He made long ago. For you see, He has, in that one grand visit, already accomplished whatever today's or tomorrow's need may demand. He has done it because of the infinite worth and purpose He sees in you and me. He stooped to reach to us because He saw so much that could be found in us if we could be recovered under the Father's purpose.

And so now, God's Holy Spirit has come to interpret for us and ignite in us all that is available to us. He has come to help us know the answer to the question, "Why have You visited us?" And it is because of the vast worth that He has intended of purpose in us that He has made the vastly magnificent condescendence in coming to visit us. And we cannot *only* survive the stress and personal failure of trials, but we can be restored to His highest purposes for us as He redeems us from our lostness and brings us under that purpose. He visits for that objective.

So speak it aloud. Declare it now: "I have been visited!" Praise Him with me: "Oh Lord, for we marvel at Your loving purpose for us, that in order to assure its fulfillment, You have paid us a visit." And as we praise Him for that, let's further thank Him that He has also promised to abide with us forever—never leaving us; never forsaking us.

THE PROBLEMS
IN THE VISIT

2

*T*hanksgiving 2003 was a day of gratitude and surprise that several hundred U. S. soldiers will never forget. Six months earlier, President George W. Bush had flown from Washington, D. C. and had landed on the aircraft carrier *USS Abraham Lincoln*. With a banner boasting the words "mission accomplished" in the background, the commander-in-chief stood on deck and spoke to the nation in a televised address, declaring that the "major combat operations" in Iraq have ended and the U.S.-led forces "have prevailed." The next words he spoke would have a level of meaning far deeper than anyone could have imagined at the time. He said the political reconstruction in Iraq would take time, and the allied troops would stay in the oil-rich country until "work is done."

For the next several months, suicide attacks and checkpoint ambushes would take a toll on American and Iraqi lives. Increased resistance to the war percolated at home. The morale among U.S. troops in Iraq was jeopardized by the bloodshed and the intensity of ongoing combat. And then came Thanksgiving Day. Shortly after 5:00 p.m. Baghdad time, Air Force One touched down at the Iraqi capital's airport. The president was then escorted to a hangar where six hundred members of the 1st Armored Division and the 82nd Airborne Division had gathered. The soldiers had been told that the U.S. civilian administrator in Iraq and the commander of coalition forces would be attending the dinner, but they had no idea another guest of honor was waiting in the wings.

As Paul Bremer, the civilian administrator, prepared to read a presidential proclamation to the troops, he said, "Let's see if we've got anybody more senior here who can read the president's Thanksgiving speech. Is there anybody back there who's more senior than I?"

Without introduction, President Bush stepped forward, wearing a U.S. Army exercise jacket. The flabbergasted GIs jumped to their feet and pumped their fists in the air. The ovation was deafening.

"I was just looking for a warm meal somewhere," Bush joked and added, "I can't think of a finer group of folks to have dinner with." He then added, "You are defending the American people from danger and we are grateful. You are defeating the terrorists here in Iraq."

Following his brief remarks and a "Happy Thanksgiving," he mingled with soldiers and took a turn on the serving line dishing out sweet potatoes and corn to those filing by to fill up their plates with turkey and the trimmings.

The unexpected visit not only caught American troops by surprise, but concern for the president's safety kept the trip cloaked in secrecy. Members of the president's staff and even some of the Secret Service were unaware of the trip. The risk associated with this amazing expression of support was high. Less than a week before, a cargo plane had been struck by an Iraqi missile and forced to land at the Baghdad airport. It was the first time a U.S. president had ever visited Iraq.

President Bush's surprise Thanksgiving visit to Baghdad was important to boost troop morale. He knew the troops needed to be encouraged. Since no phone call or email could take the place of a personal visit, the commander-in-chief was determined to show up in person. It was an amazing picture of one accustomed to being served taking up the role of servant despite the cost.

On a much deeper level, the Creator's arrival was all the more necessary. A visit was needed. Mankind needed God's care and help, despite the cost.

Mankind needed God's care and help, despite the cost.

What we read in the last chapter verifies our human need for a divine visit. But there was another need, and it is important that we study that need to gain a complete understanding and appreciation of the visit.

You see, the other need was the Visitor's.

IF SOMEONE IS GOING TO PAY A VISIT, THEN THERE are difficulties which may not be apparent to us but which the visitor knows he must resolve. What is obvious to us is that anyone who is going to pay a visit will need to give a certain amount of time and effort to go to the place of his visit. Unless these demands are met, neither the visit, nor the benefits of the visit, are possible.

A telephone conversation may allow us to share and talk briefly with others, but a visit is another matter, for then someone actually has to come to give the time. And we value the gift of that investment—time and energy given to more fully understand our situation and genuinely care for us. And so it was that the giving of time and going personally were the essential requirements for our heavenly Visitor to meet, both for His purposes and for our needs.

But here is a problem: It is one thing to imagine the president of the United States giving up his Thanksgiving meal with his own family and leaving the White House to travel to Iraq, but when we try to imagine the sacrifices the Creator made to arrange His visit, our minds can't begin to understand. In the Visitor's need to go to a specific place and spend a specific amount of time, there are difficulties that go well beyond the inconveniences a human visitor must overcome. This heavenly Visitor faces confining factors that are contrary to His very being.

For example, since the One who is giving time and going on a personal visit is God Himself, to explain how He made His visit confronts us with enormous difficulties that are rooted in God's very nature.

1. We are speaking of the Eternal One giving time, but He is timeless.

2. We are speaking of the Omnipresent One going to one place on a solitary planet within His own creation. But God is everywhere. His being transcendent of time and transcendent of space present

contradictions that defy easy analysis, and they exceed our general supposition, because human concepts of God are usually far too small.

3. We tend to think of Him on human terms within human definitions that haven't been sufficiently expanded to include His full "God-ness."

Dear one, God is not simply a larger-than-life humanoid. He strongly asserts this in His Word. He emphasizes the contrast between man's limitations and fallibility and His transcendence and perfection. Reading from Isaiah we find: "For as the heavens are higher than the earth, so are My ways higher than your ways, and My thoughts than your thoughts" (55:9).

From the book of Numbers: "God is not a man, that He should lie" (23:19).

From the book of Job: "As for the Almighty, we cannot find Him; He is excellent in power, in judgment and abundant justice; He does not oppress" (37:23).

From the Scriptures, we read that God is not manlike—not even supermanlike. He clearly states that He is wholly "other" from us, on another plane entirely. And though that should humble us, He doesn't say it to humiliate us. Nor does He declare His exceeding difference from us by making us grovel before His throne. But we do need to see something of these dimensions of His greatness to fully appreciate the investment He makes in visiting us.

Here is the Eternal One planning to give us time; the Omnipresent One preparing to confine Himself to one place; and the Omniscient One who, knowing all things, still comes to learn of life on the terms of His own creation. This condescension is not easily accomplished.

To understand the problems inherent in God's confinement of Himself to time, we have to think clearly about eternity. Too many of us tend to view eternity from a linear perspective, as though it is only the sum of the indefinite past and the infinite future. But to view eternity this way is to omit the present. Now our human reason tends to separate eternity from the present era of human experience, somehow trying to crowd or to sandwich time into a parenthesis between two eternities. There is the eternal past, the eternal future, and then stuck right here in the middle is the period of time as though eternity paused for the exercise of time. And then when time concludes, eternity resumes. But this is not a biblical perspective.

From such a limited point of view, eternity is both unreal and irrelevant. It becomes a philosophical blind spot that puts the todays of our lives in a space between the two eternities, yet insulated from them. By such reasoning, today becomes a temporary zone, aside and apart from the eternal, where our daily existence occurs. But time and eternity should not be confused by such compartmental-izing, as though time refers only to where we live now, and eternity refers to something either remotely past or distantly future.

The truth of God's Word is that time—our present mo-ment—is an immediate part of eternity. Eternity is now surrounding us. Eternity encompasses time as an ocean encompasses a water drop. All the ocean's drops are ever present; they are now. And so from God's eternal perspec-tive, both the future and the past are now. They are occur-ring simultaneously; an ongoing process.

Time—our present moment—is an immediate part of eternity.

Seem staggering to the imagination? I should hope so, because we are dealing with God's perspective which does transcend ours. And the objective is to see that the call for the Visitor to leave eter-nity as it were, to confine Himself to time, to reduce Himself to the limits of our tiny space of processing life is an overwhelmingly humbling thing when we realize He would do it for us. Of course, this grandeur of our God that exceeds time and space is why Christ is called the Alpha and the Omega—the beginning and the ending—for by His eternal nature, He encompasses everything before time, of time, and beyond it.

But this isn't true with us. Mankind is locked in a time-space continuum, limited to our one drop of the drops in the ocean, so to speak; to this immediate moment—just now, today, this instant. We are always looking back to the before or forward to the after. And yet our present is not excluded, isolated, or separate from eternity; it is within it. We are within eternity, but not beyond it.

Now God is both. He fills eternity and exists above and beyond it. He also fills all time, including Himself in every present moment, while at the same time infinitely transcending it. And it is this transcendent quality of His eternal nature that brings one of our Visitor's problems into focus.

YOU SEE, IF GOD, WHO HAS NO LIMITATIONS, IS TO visit people who are locked in the limits of time, He must confine Himself to the "now" within the vastness of eternity. And He can do this only if He will consent to a proposition which, by reason of His eternal nature, is a step of incredible, incalculable condescension. He must restrict Himself to a time segment. And in doing so, He must somehow temporarily set aside that aspect of His being which we call "Eternal."

How can it be done? And yet the second person of the Godhead, Jesus the Son, accepts the restriction of a thirty-three-year earth time measure to accomplish this visit.

How can we help but be humbled by this Visitor's willingness?

Why, when He can create a galaxy by merely speaking a word, would He stoop to the limits of time to do His work?

Why not accomplish man's salvation in an instant, with a word or a momentary action? Why not remain without the time-space continuum and simply order that His salvation penetrate it by a divine edict?

Why? Because without time, without a season spent in visiting, He would neither gain the experience through full identification of the ones He seeks to save—experience that makes Him sensitive to their pain, their hurt, their need—nor would He gain the confidence of their love. Mankind needed time to know Him. So He chose to take time to be with them, and in that choice, the Visitor allows His eternal being to be temporarily walled within the restrictions of time.

BUT GOD NOT ONLY CAME WITHIN TIME, THE VISITOR must also find a way to confine Himself within space.

For the Omnipresent One to come and be with us, the visited ones, He had to become visible and touchable. He could not simply say, "I am everywhere, so reach out. I am there." He can and does say this after His coming. But to first establish contact, the Visitor has to visit us on terms we can see and understand. He who fills the heavens now stoops to earth. He who can span the universe faster than the speed of light

In consenting to visit us, Christ placed omniscience into the schoolroom of human experience.

has willingly limited Himself to the pace at which human feet tread earth's dusty roads. The people He had chosen to visit could not fathom "omnipresence," nor could they touch "spirit." So, the Visitor willingly confined Himself in terms of space to come to us.

WITHIN THE LIMITS OF TIME AND SPACE, HE ALSO accepted additional terms. In consenting to visit us, Christ placed omniscience into the schoolroom of human experience. All knowledge comes to learn of what man endures, lives through, and suffers. He who knows all, acknowledged His desire to learn and to discover human pain in a human body, to feel human disappointment with human emotions, to suffer human misunderstanding.

He might simply have asserted His perception of these human sensations. His justice would have been no less righteous. He would not have been less loving, less holy, or less God had He never submitted Himself to these things.

But He did submit to them. And in coming, He accepted these restrictions.

Remember how the commander-in-chief of our armed forces went to visit his soldiers on the battlefield so he could experience firsthand the challenges they face while far from home? How remarkable to acknowledge what the Divine Visitor did for us.

Hebrews 5:8 reads: "Though He was a Son, yet He learned obedience by the things which He suffered."

No wonder the psalmist marvels, "What is man that You visit him?"

The Eternal One confined Himself to time.

The Omnipresent One confined Himself to one place.

And the Omniscient One has chosen to learn the frailty of humanity.

WHO IS THIS VISITOR?

3

*D*uring his reign, King Hussein of Jordan was once reputed to have left the royal residence without security, camouflaged as a commoner. Borrowing a taxi, he drove around the city of Amman listening to what was on the minds of random passengers. He realized the only way to truly experience the plight of the people in his kingdom was to lay aside his royal garments, take on the appearance of his subjects, and mingle with them.

King Abdullah II, who ascended the throne after his father's death in 1999, followed his father's example. The thirty-seven-year-old leader of the Hashemite kingdom disguised himself on several occasions in order to mingle with his subjects. As with his more famous father, his rationale was the same: to understand his constituents in order to better serve them. Dressing up like an old Arab man, the young king once appeared in public with a fake white beard. He wore a traditional Jordanian "Kufiah" and white dress.

The king disguised himself as an old man on another occasion when he visited a hospital. Another time he resorted to his father's famous escapade by circulating around Amman behind the wheel of a taxicab. Yet one other time he passed himself off as a television reporter covering a story at a duty-free shop.

One day while wearing a disguise, the king walked around two government buildings without security and without being noticed. On the day of this clandestine experiment, he engaged people in conversation while waiting in a long line and listened to their thoughts. Amazingly, even though King Abdullah II spent nearly two hours that day visiting with his subjects, no one recognized him. Those near him realized something was up, however, when they saw him approach his official car surrounded by security. According to published reports, employees in the Jordanian government buildings began looking more closely at the faces of people who lingered in the lobby or passed by on the sidewalks. They never knew when they might meet their king in disguise. One who resembled an ordinary visitor might be anything but.

Both King Hussein and his son clothed themselves in the garb of commoners in order to experience what life was like outside of their royal home on the common level. Even though it meant temporarily laying aside their recognizable identity, they were willing to do it in order to better serve their subjects. Sound familiar? We have a theological word for this kind of ignoble, self-effacing conduct: *incarnation*.

The Divine Visitor—the One who would make this visit—who would go through this condescension is named in Hebrews 2:9: "But we see Jesus, who was made a little lower than the angels." In those few words, we are given the fact of Jesus' condescension.

The word *condescension* could be objectionable to some. It can sound as though God were patronizing man. We must avoid the ignorance or presumption of such objections, and a precise assessment of who the Visitor is will help us do that.

He is far more than a monarch of a Middle Eastern kingdom. When we see more completely the uniqueness of His nature, we will be better equipped to escape the potential arrogance which entraps those ingrained with pagan philosophy or humanistic theology.

You see, man-sized ideas are not enough. Pagan and popular ideas about God are everywhere. As in the ancient *The Odyssey* and *The Iliad*, popularized views of God are heard today; notions which reduce Him to little more than

an oversized human. In varied ways, God is recast in twen-
tieth-century terms from the hip "Big Daddy" to the deper-
sonalized "Force." This is little more than a verbal retooling
of the characters in the legends of Greece, Rome, or
Scandinavia where "gods" were merely immortal men with
superhuman powers. And yet they were humanly unpre-
dictable, moody, immoral, and vindictive, with one twist—
being immortal and having virtually unlimited power, they
ruled in might—unjust, vengeful, and brutal. This broadly
defines the average man's view of God today, even if that
"God" is one they only call "Fate."

Careless thinking and general ignorance introduce so
many distorted views of the living God that it is a small
wonder that so many prefer agnosticism or atheism—
denying God's existence outright. It seems a sounder option
than to believe in a God defined by humanized theology.
Cheap theology breeds unbelief and one cannot blame the
person who does not believe in a God like that.

I wouldn't either.

But to think clearly of Jesus—the One made lower than
the angels—we must understand something of the dimension of His nature before He was made lower. This perspective builds a faith which senses man's high destiny and
purpose, since it perceives the true dimension of the person
who came. When we see the full worth of the person of

Jesus, we begin to see what it was worth to Him to pay mankind a visit; not to mention what man was worth to God that He would extend and expend the life of His Son.

Hebrews 1:1–3 introduces us to several facets of the glory of this Visitor:

> God, who at various times and in various ways spoke in time past to the fathers by the prophets, has in these last days spoken to us by His Son, whom He has appointed heir of all things, through whom also He made the worlds; who being the brightness of His glory and the express image of His person, and upholding all things by the word of His power, when He had by Himself purged our sins, sat down at the right hand of the Majesty on high.

Those verses declare that God has conclusively spoken to us through His Son. Jesus Christ is God's message to man. Jesus is not only a message of God's love, but He communicated God's likeness—that is, what He is really like. A careful summary of His attributes is important to help us form our perceptions of the Visitor, His interest in us, and the worth He places upon us.

Jesus Christ is God's message to man.

Consider these things.

1. He is "heir of all things" (Hebrews 1:2). It has pleased
God that all things will ultimately dwell in Christ—that
everything in creation is bequeathed to, or willed to, Him. It
will ultimately belong to Him. No stipulations are made as to
the requirements He must meet to receive this. The visit is
not demanded—only requested. This One, Christ, volunteering to bear all the humbling confinements the visit
requires, is the One to whom all things have already been
promised. "It is My will," the Father has said, "that all the
cosmos be His—My Son's."

So why then this remarkable condescension? The staggering truth is that it is for one reason: His visit is in our
interest to allow for the possibility that we—you and I—
might share with Him in that cosmic inheritance. Romans
8:15–17 declares it: It is the will of the Father that through
Christ we become joint heirs, partners in the inheritance
the Father has willed the Son.

2. We have also just read that it is through Him,
through Christ, that all the worlds were made. The partnership within the Trinity at creation is an interesting
study. God the Father willed all things to be. The Son spoke
all things into existence as the Father had willed, and the

Holy Spirit's power was the energy by which all things were brought into being. The full Trinity, manifest in creation, shows it is the product of the Father's will, the Son's word, and the Spirit's work. John writes in his Gospel:

> In the beginning was the Word, and the Word was with God, and the Word was God. . . . All things were made through Him, and without Him nothing was made that was made (John 1:1, 3).

Don't let it escape your understanding, dear one. The Visitor was present at the founding of creation, yet He chose to become a part of it Himself.

3. Hebrews 1:3 notes that He is the express image of God. The Greek noun *karakter* (translated image) was commonly used in the ancient world to describe the figure struck on a coin when minted. By its engraved authenticity and its stamped value, a coin declares its worth and its genuineness, and so it is today.

So it is with Jesus, for when we look at Him we are seeing the full worthiness and the true magnificence of God. In Christ, all confusion as to what God is like is cleared up. Jesus is His "express image," indeed the genuine article, the Son of the God above all gods. He is not a fluke of humanity or a human with divine genius. He is divine in His entirety, notwithstanding His having adopted man's humanity with all its limits, except for sin.

Now, think back to the king of Jordan. Although he was robed in the street clothes of an ordinary citizen, he was no less a king while surreptitiously engaging passersby in conversation. The same is true with God. Appearing on earth in human skin, He was no less than He was in His invisible form when He created the cosmos.

4. The text notes that He upholds all things by the word of His power. This is to say that He who spoke all things into existence continues by the sheer power of His creative word to sustain them in existence. Thus, the authority and the almightiness invested in the words our Visitor speaks will be of another quality. Just as He who has spoken creation into existence and sustains it in continuum, when He speaks a promise it can be believed. When He declares a goal concerning His work and His will for His own redeemed, in your life or in mine, we can depend on His bringing it about. Loved one, if He can sustain all creation by His own word, we can rest assured He'll see us through when He says He will. Hallelujah!

If He can sustain all creation, He'll see us through when He says He will.

5. Hebrews 1:3 says He Himself purged our sins. The statement "by Himself purged our sins" means both alone—that is, by Himself without the aid of others; without the need of added worth—but also that it was at the expense of Himself. He made Himself the price for our sins, pouring out His own blood.

Further, the value of this payment is sufficient to satisfy the immeasurable, incredible debt of human sin. And it is because of this sufficiency that these words are spoken: "He . . . sat down at the right hand of the Majesty on high" (Hebrews 1:3). When He does this, He is making a divine announcement: "My work is done; it is finished."

The high quality, the peerless character, and the eternal significance of our Visitor are all shown in the completion of His assignment. Upon His finishing with that task, having visited us in a form "a little lower than the angels" (Hebrews 2:9), He is to return to be with His Father on high.

But during that visit, He was killed.

The process, simply stated in the phrase "when He had by Himself purged our sins" (Hebrews 1:3), involved His death, and He submitted to it willingly. He came as a Visitor to show the care, the love of God, knowing that in coming it would involve His dying, and His dying at the hands of the very ones He came to visit. He came to accomplish salvation. It was included in the visitation plans.

But man didn't know of that willingness or of that plan. He only functioned in the limits of his own blindness, bondage, and capacity for folly. And so it was, dear ones, that we killed the Visitor—this one of eternal, regal, noble stature. And He refused retaliation, for He had accomplished the high objective of His coming. He had visited us with salvation.

Inquiring into the Unfathomable

$\mathcal{E}$very March since 1973, the Iditarod has taken place in Alaska. It's a most unusual race. It doesn't involve race cars or bicycles or iron-man runners. It's a 1,100-mile long sled dog race. Sixty mushers, each with a team of sixteen dogs pulling a sled, leave Anchorage headed for the finish line on Front Street in Nome. Braving blizzards, whiteouts, wind storms, and treacherous trails, these mushers and their dog teams follow a predetermined route that snakes through mountain passes, river deltas, windswept tundra, and atop the frozen Bering Sea. The grueling race can take anywhere from nine days to three weeks.

The Iditarod Trail Sled Dog Race (nicknamed "The Last Great Race") is actually an annual event intended to commemorate a far more important race that took place in arctic Alaska in the early part of the last century. On January 21, 1925, the lives of countless children in Nome were at stake. An epidemic of diphtheria had broken out in the legendary gold rush city. The townsfolk were greatly concerned because there was not an adequate supply of antitoxin to treat the infected children. Unless some additional medicine could be found and transported to Nome, the results would be devastating.

Dr. Curtis Welch, Nome's lone physician, frantically telegraphed Fairbanks, Anchorage, Seward, and Juneau, asking for help. The initial response was not encouraging. Dr. Welch swallowed hard and hoped the prayers of Christian families in town would be answered. At last, word came from the state's largest city—300,000 units of the serum had been located at a hospital in Anchorage. It was the only serum in the entire state.

But finding the lifesaving serum was only half the challenge. Once it was located, Dr. Welch had to figure out a way to transport the antitoxin to Nome in the shortest time possible. That was no easy task due to the fact that Nome's position on the coastline of the Seward Peninsula is extremely remote. No railroads or conventional roads linked the small community with the rest of the state. What few airplanes there were in Anchorage were unavailable and since the Bering Sea was frozen eight months of the year, there was no access by boat. The only means of getting the serum to the dying children was by dog team. Weather-permitting, dogs were dependable. But they typically travel only six miles an hour.

The decision was made to transport the serum by rail to the town of Nenana near Fairbanks. The 300,000 units were packed in an insulated container and loaded onto an overnight train. Once the serum arrived in Nenana, a distance of 674 miles remained. Because it took the musher who delivered the mail a month to cover that stretch of miles, it was decided a relay team of mushers would be required. The first musher took the insulated cylinder of serum fifty-two miles where he passed the lifesaving baton to the second musher who traveled thirty-one miles.

From musher to musher the relay continued until a total of twenty sled dog drivers cooperated to get the needed medicine to Nome. Despite brutal conditions including blinding snowstorms and temperatures dropping as low as −64° F the serum arrived in Nome at 5:40 a.m. on February 2nd, barely a week after leaving Anchorage and 127 hours after departing Nenana. Thanks to the cooperative effort of individuals who were willing to risk their own lives and those of their dogs to bridge a near impossible gap, a sure-tragedy had been averted.

A few people had committed to go the distance, no matter how far or how hard. Because of those who orchestrated the novel plan, the source of salvation was not hindered by miles to be covered.

The distance spanned in getting the medicine to that remote village on the Bering Sea pales in comparison to the distance God overcame in order to reach us with the only solution that could save our souls. But that Visitor had to be made "a little lower than the angels," and that brings us to a difficult place in attempting to understand His coming.

What is the distance from God to angels, or from angels to man?

THERE IS THE STAGGERING TRUTH OF SUCH condescension itself—God, lower than His own creatures. But even more, we're overwhelmed by the fact that we have no point of reference as to the degree of stooping or condescending this represents. What is the distance from God to angels, or from angels to man? There are no hints, no criteria, and no benchmarks by which we can measure. The Serum Run trail, from Nenana to Nome, can be painstakingly measured with a dogsled and an odometer: 674 miles. But how can we measure the positional distance between the role or ranks of creatures? We're placed in the position of inquiring into the unfathomable—the measureless expanse between the persons of God the Creator, and man the creature, below angels, another order of creature.

To begin, the one thing we can readily understand is there is a vast difference between the Creator and His creation. For example, I know the man who built the pulpit from which I teach and preach. It's a very fine demonstration of my friend's craftsmanship. It tells you something of his skill and creativity, but there's no real comparison between the artisan and the lectern—the pulpit. There's an immeasurable difference in distance between the man and his work. If he were to stand alongside his handiwork, who could draw a valid assessment of the relative worth of either man or pulpit?

So when we begin with the Creator of all things, in an attempt to measure the space between His being and His creation, there seems to be no way to comprehend the distance. And in our seeing Jesus as being made a little lower than the angels, we face the same dilemma. Like the arctic trail, where there are no mileposts or checkpoints, there seems to be no point of reference or comparison. No mathematics, economics, or geometrics exist for us to begin to develop an appreciation of the vast distance God spanned when He became man.

What foundation can we give for our values? Well, this problem deserves our attention, for we're dealing with more than speculation about the grandeur of God from man's viewpoint. We're also dealing with the value of man from God's perspective. Our inability to precisely and intelligently assess God's greatness also peculiarly inhibits our own ability to place a proper value on ourselves, and it's precisely that value which He saw in us that caused Him to span that cosmic chasm to pay us a visit. That consideration is important for us; not for self-congratulation or for a contrived inflation of our human worth, but so that an accurate evaluation of man's potential and perspective purpose might be made. God spanned the universe that separated us from Him, not to capture, but to win a race of kings.

Capturing this viewpoint will alter our attitudes concerning the greatness of God's salvation. It's an indispensable need for any of us because if we have a small perspective on the nature of the Visitor, then we miss the magnitude of His condescension, we will miss seeing the enormity of His care for us and the grandeur of His plan for us. So intelligently understanding His greatness allows for the true understanding that appreciates the phrase, "so great a salvation" (Hebrews 2:3). We begin to see the real grounds for our placing the value that God has placed on us. We are the object of God's visit, and this standard of evaluating human worth excels the best efforts of humanistic philosophy which must depend on its own self-assessment to establish values. Man's philosophical base is a closed system that imposes severe limits that reduce man's intrinsic value—at best, cheapening him, and at worst, obliterating his purpose and destiny.

At best, humanized systems make man out to be an ascending god with virtually unlimited inherent potential for becoming. But this view cheapens man's actual worth, because while it affirms those possibilities, it provides no better leverage than man himself to accomplish them.

Age upon age has already verified the inability of human flesh to catapult man into his new age of self-realization. Thus, this proposition insults human intelligence by attempting to sell philosophical froth again and again. At worst, human systems cast man as either an advanced animal or a sophisticated mixture of chemicals boiled to a new stage of attainment, intellectually, sociologically, and technologically. This view obliterates man's highest destiny for it proposes nothing of spirit transcending the drive of an animal and nothing of timelessness exceeding the duration of inert matter. It's only when such static states of thought are confronted and corrected by the revelation of God's eternal Word and the truth in Jesus Christ that the true value of the human being is most intelligently understood: Man's highest potential and eternal destiny can be seen and realized.

Our investigation then, our inquiry into the unfathomable, is for practical reasons. A deepened understanding of Christ's condescension will increase our sense of man's distinct destiny and our own personal present sense of purpose and worth. Such dynamic faith born of clear-headed insight into eternal issues will begin to alter our priorities. Praise toward God will increase. Self-esteem on God's terms can rise and the spirit of faith will soar. And all of this flows from the uplifting certainty that the One who has reached so far to touch me is certainly not going to fail me now. He is absolutely committed to seeing me through to the full realization of His purpose for my existence. If He stooped so far to visit, it's that He may realize the lifting unto His high purpose and destiny. He will achieve it.

There are two questions to resolve then. Increasing our realization of God's purpose will be easier if we resolve these points:

1. Why was Jesus made lower than angels?

2. Can we conceive of the reality that this did, indeed, happen?

Why was Christ made lower than the angels? The biblical answer is direct and absolute. It was planned so that He could experience suffering and death. Unless He becomes a man, He could not do either. There is no other way to pay the price of salvation, no other way to release mankind at every point of his bondage. We will examine these details further, but it's enough for now to say it all had to take place on these terms and in human flesh.

Secondly, can we conceive of the reality that Christ was made a little lower than the angels? Is there any vantage point we can gain that will allow us to more appreciably perceive the distance the Visitor traversed? It's a tough problem. Where can I stand to gain even a glimpse of the distance between deity and man? All we do know in this present order of things is, first, man is lower than angels, and second, both are lower than God. But how from those propositions can I deduce the

Where can I stand to gain even a glimpse of the distance between deity and man?

extent of His condescension? To attempt an answer, allow me to offer an illustration which is wholly consistent with the spirit of God's Word.

As I described the Serum Run of 1925 at the beginning of this chapter, you no doubt were able to visualize that courageous relay race on the windswept, ice-packed trail. In your imagination, you vicariously experienced the journey. Now, I invite you to an imaginary trip that might help us toward some notion of the degree of Christ being made lower to visit us. Take with me, if you will, an excursion into eternity.

BEGIN PLEASE, BY SUPPOSING YOURSELF TO HAVE already been resurrected into the presence of the Lord Jesus. He's come for His church. She's already celebrated her reunion with her Lord. The great wedding feast has already occurred, and in this excursion into the realm of timelessness, ages upon ages have already rolled by when one day there comes a moment. The Lord Jesus Himself calls for you to come to Him at His throne. You appear in His presence and with joy bow before Him inquiring of His will. He responds by inviting you to join Him on a journey.

"Where are we going, Lord?" you ask.

He replies, "To a place—a place in Father's universe. Come."

Suddenly, having traveled with your Lord at the speed of thought, you find yourself standing somewhere in the midst of the enormity of space looking down on a small planet. He stands beside you, silently observing the orb and then slowly extends His hand and points to it.

"This is the place of which I spoke," He says. "The place where I wanted to bring you."

"And for what purpose, my Lord?"

"Because I wish to talk with you about the creatures who dwell there. And from here you can see the place of their habitation."

You look from His face to the small world below. Distance prohibits any sign or notion of the beings who inhabit it.

The Lord continues: "It is important for you to understand what has transpired there before I ask a question of you."

"What question, my Lord?"

"I want to ask your feelings about what action might be taken."

You look at the Lord of Glory with curiosity, and He explains the creatures of that world are creatures you and I knew as dogs on the world where we once lived.

He pauses pensively then adds, "Father made them, you know."

Again, you look down upon that speck in space, reminded somehow by the gentleness in the Savior's voice that the infinite power behind the creation of all things is also the infinite lover of all that He has created.

As He continues speaking of the animals on the planet below, the Master observes, "Of course, I know that mankind has sometimes affectionately considered dogs almost human, but they aren't. They are not even close to man in Father's order. For you," He says, turning to look deep into your eyes, "you are the only ones We have made in Our image."

The awareness of the uniqueness of man's destiny and the high honor of his having been redeemed moves you to worship, but the Lord is still speaking.

"Dogs are of entirely another order; as different from man as fallen man was different from God."

You nod to Him with understanding, knowing now something of that dimensional difference since you have been in the eternal realm for ages long passed.

"We are here," the Savior goes on, "because something very terrible has happened on that small planet. As it now stands, not one of these creatures remembers how they were first created. Despite what several teams of them accomplished in Alaska a century ago, they neither understand how they were intended to live nor recall their place in Father's created order, for Father creates nothing without purpose. Their tiny consciousnesses have been damaged. The understanding of purpose that Father and I engraved in every creature's awareness has been confused in these. They have become twisted within, and now they have all taken to deadly and vicious practices. Like the dogs you and I have seen on earth, they often travel in packs and . . ." He pauses, sighing painfully, ". . . and they fight with one another."

He speaks haltingly, seeming to suffer their pain. "At times they rip and tear at each other. They seem to have lost whatever they knew of their appointed design."

As He continues, the Great Shepherd of the Universe seems to groan. "With this as it is, there is nothing they can do for themselves. They have no way to become again what Father meant for them to be, even as animals at their beginning."

The look on His face stirs your compassion. You feel a heightened sensitivity to the Father's loving desire that all His creation—from stars and suns to donkeys and dogs—enjoy what He intended for each in their distinct purpose and that they be fulfilled in it.

Then Jesus says, "I have brought you here to see this and ask you if . . . if you would consider going to them and explaining that they were created for something far better. I brought you on this excursion to see if you would go and tell them that when the order of any part of Father's creation is distorted, it truly grieves Him. Would you help Us show them Father's love in a way they can understand? If that were done, they might return to their intended order and stop their hateful and deadly ways." He pauses, looking at you quietly, then asks, "Would you go to them for Us?"

Your heart feels the pulse of the divine love which has redeemed you, and you answer with a hesitant but honest question: "I want to do Your will, oh Lord, but how shall I go?"

"And in this imaginary trip I've invited you to take with Me," the Lord Jesus replies, "that's the most difficult part in My asking you, you see, because they will not be able to understand anything other than a dog."

It suddenly comes to you. "A dog?"

The full, crushing implications of His request descend upon you, for it is a request, not a mandate. Then He turns to face you and says, "You also need to know this. If you go, some of them will come to understand and the goal of their created purpose will be restored. But only some, not all of them, will respond favorably." There's a pause. "As I told you, they have become wild and some of them in their wildness and viciousness will turn on you and . . ." He seems reluctant to finish but after a moment He goes on, ". . . and they will kill you."

You turn to look toward a lost race of brute creatures, a breed of animals on a lonely planet in a darkened corner of the universe, then slowly your eyes return to His, and He speaks again. "If you choose to go, I make you this promise: Your living and dying there will not be the end, but I will bring you back to be with Me to enjoy the delights of the glory in Our presence. But for just a season, in order that those damaged creatures may understand Father's intended order for them, will you go?"

And it is here that we conclude our imagined scenario. Its purpose has been to say this, dear friend: I have a great deal of love for human beings and even a great deal of compassion for a wounded animal, but it's extremely difficult for me to imagine myself, for however noble a reason, stooping to the animal kingdom to become a dog. Something of the weight of what God did presses upon my soul as I measure the difference of the essential being between beasts and humans. How can the space between these two created orders be gauged? I can hardly imagine being asked to span such a gap by allowing the essential nature of my being to be altered to such a degree as to make possible my existence on an equal plane with a dog. But I also hasten to affirm that the span between different created orders—between the human and the animal kingdom—is infinitely smaller than the span between the order of the Creator and His own creatures.

And yet there was a day long ago when the Father said, "Son, You know that some will hear the truth and walk in Our way, but if You go, some of them will turn on You, and they will kill You. Will You go?"

In the light of this truth that Christ consented to be made lower than the angels and suffer death, I invite you, as the writer of our text says in Hebrews 2:9, to see Jesus. And in looking at Him, consider the richness of the great salvation He brought us—reaching so far because He loves so much. What high destiny He sees in us, and it's one we only begin to apprehend when we grasp, at least in part, the degree of His condescension.

Let your soul praise Him with me, would you?

Oh marvelous and mighty Father,

God, thank You for visiting me.

Thank You for sending Jesus, Your Son.

Dear Lord Jesus, thank You for condescending to

become one of us.

Thank You for Your coming to touch,

to teach, and to save.

Holy Spirit, enlarge my understanding of the scope of

Jesus' salvation, His coming, His suffering,

His wounds, His blood, and His death that I may see

beyond tears to perceive the dynamic

and the life You convey to me by those means.

In Jesus' name, Amen.

THE VISITOR'S
SUFFERING

5

I Thirst

Is it possible that He who claimed to be living water . . .
Is it possible that He who said,
"Come unto Me and drink . . ."
Is it possible that He who told the Samaritan woman
that He had water she knew nothing about . . .
Is it possible that this Man could mouth the words,
"I thirst?"

And because He did, the incarnation
message of Christmas
is voiced in this human cry of Good Friday.
Jesus the divine Creator of life
is now subject to the creation

and the creature's basic needs.

Yes, Jesus, the Son of God, actually needed water.

For six hours He hung from a calloused cross

on a hot barren hill

beneath a darkened middle-eastern sky.

He was bleeding profusely and losing vital body fluids.

What is more,

without sleep the night before,

without food or drink, He had been tortured, teased,

and tried before a tribunal

before the crucifixion had even begun.

His lips were parched. His tongue swollen

as He managed to blurt out His human thirst . . .

A thirst that spoke of His total identification with all our

needs,

drives,

hopes,

and sufferings.

Jesus' physical thirst only symbolized the deeper thirsts

that every human being who ever lived has felt:

the thirst for companionship,

the thirst for acceptance,

the thirst for immortality,

the thirst for end to suffering,

and most importantly

the thirst for relationship with God.
Augustine said it centuries ago:
"Thou has made me for thyself, O God,
And I am restless till I rest in Thee."
But the Psalmist said it long before Augustine:
"As the deer pants for flowing streams,
so thirsts my soul for Thee, O God."
A restlessness,
a panting,
a thirst to end all thirsts,
a thirst no water,
no wine,
no gall could ever quench.
And for once Jesus knew that desire of all ages Himself.
As the bearer of all sin,
of all people,
of all time,
Jesus knew the separation and desperation
that all creation has known apart from God.
And He cried, "I thirst."

The Baby of Bethlehem,
The Christ of the cross
knows the creature's cage.
He's acquainted with our pain,
our pressures,

our panic,
our plight apart from the Father.
And because He's been there,
He knows how to quench our thirst.

—GREG ASIMAKOUPOULOS

*I*n this poem by Greg Asimakoupoulos, we are provided a word picture of our Lord's passion. Beyond the vivid images of Mel Gibson's movie, we are given a canvas rich with descriptive phrases that illustrate why the sinless Son of God suffered by visiting our sinful planet. Beyond the physical torment of His beatings and crucifixion, we see a portrait of what it meant for the Creator's innocent spirit to be imprisoned in the creature's cage. We see the spiritual torture of bearing the sin of the world in His soul. But we also witness a remarkable study of this Visitor's awesome ability to empathize with and redeem the human condition.

LET'S LOOK TOGETHER AND READ THE SCRIPTURES that will guide us in considering how He suffered:

For it was fitting for Him, for whom are all things and by whom are all things, in bringing many sons to glory, to make the captain of their salvation perfect through sufferings. . . . Therefore, in all things He had to be made like His brethren, that He might be a merciful and faithful High Priest in things pertaining to God, to make propitiation for the sins of the people. For in that He Himself has suffered, being tempted, He is able to aid those who are tempted (Hebrews 2:10, 17–18).

Let's also read Hebrews 5:7–9:

. . . who, in the days of His flesh, when He had offered up prayers and supplications, with vehement cries and tears to Him who was able to save Him from death, and was heard because of His godly fear, though He was a Son, yet He learned obedience by the things which He suffered. And having been perfected, He became the author of eternal salvation to all who obey Him.

What if Jesus had lived in virtual obscurity all His life? What if His real identity had remained absolutely hidden, until one day He suddenly announced, "I am God!"?

And what if, over the next few weeks, He preached several memorable sermons and performed a series of remarkable miracles to verify His divinity to onlookers? Then, without prior warning, declared, "I will die to save all mankind."

And what if His words one day so inflamed the anger of

a mob that they killed Him instantly, and He died the victim of violence—a death virtually without pain, struck down in fury?

What if there had been no years of bone-wearying, itinerant ministry, no bewildering rejection, no embittered accusations, no mock trial, no jeering, no beatings, no crown of thorns, no crucifixion, no suffering, none at all— suddenly exterminated?

It might have happened that way, you know. After all, the type of lamb that was slain on the altar of the Old Testament—the perfect symbol of the coming Lamb of God—was slain with just one rapid slit of the throat. The Old Testament sacrifice of animals didn't require agony, didn't involve brutality—only death. There was, then, a ritual precedent for the substitutionary sacrifice of a dying lamb—but not necessarily for a suffering one.

The lamb is a means of restoration as well as redemption.

Why then, did the prophecy of Isaiah call a suffering Messiah, ensuring that, in coming as the Visitor, Jesus Christ would endure a lifetime of struggle, loneliness, stress, temptation, pain, and anguish? And why should the visit require Him to die a slow, torturous death of crucifixion, rather than one of instant, painless demise? The answer is that this Lamb is a means of restoration as well as redemption, and His sufferings are an essential part of that mission.

In Asimakoupoulos's poem, we see the meaning behind the morbidity of Jesus' drawn out agony. "And because He's been there, He knows how to quench our thirst." But that has not always been recognized historically as the reason why it pleased God for His servant to suffer. Let's consider it now. Consider the suffering Savior.

THROUGHOUT THE HISTORY OF THE CHURCH, THE sufferings of Christ have often been depicted in such a way as to suggest God is saying to us, "The reason I had My Son suffer so much is that I wanted you always to remember and to be saddened by what your sin did." This mood is portrayed in much of the medieval and contemporary religious art forms, and it dominates the climate of many ecclesiastical rituals as though to say, "You hurt God, and don't you ever forget it."

Now, there is an understandable and appropriate sense of shame and regret that should come to our hearts when we meditate on what our Lord endured for our salvation. But God's objective in Christ's suffering was not to produce that emotion of suffering in us. The suffering of Christ has more to do with our release and restoration, indeed, our joy, than with any divinely intended summons to feel shame.

Hebrews 2:10 says that through Christ's sufferings there was a perfecting; that is, a completion of His Saviorhood. That tells us this: The Son of God submitted to a plan that would include a lifetime of the same kind of suffering that you and I experience. And this plan would have something to do with setting us free from the oppressive power of that suffering. Christ didn't appear to merely share our plight.

Perhaps you've heard of the father who had his head shaved so that his eight-year-old daughter who lost her hair from chemotherapy wouldn't feel alone in the physical dimension of her cancer fight. What Jesus did is far more than cosmetic. His plan to enter our suffering with an eye to relieve it is more like the mother who gave up half her liver so that her son, who needed the life-giving transplant, could have one. In that case, both mother and son faced major surgery and recovery. They both faced the risks of complications, rejection, and infection. But in order to find a cure for her son, this middle-aged mother expressed her love through a willingness to enter into his suffering and gave up something of herself in the process.

Hebrews 4:15 says: "For we do not have a High Priest who cannot sympathize with our weaknesses."

We all need someone who understands our feelings, our vulnerability both to emotional and physical pain. We need someone who identifies with the utter weakness of our flesh, especially before the ferocious onslaught of fear, doubt, anger, and lust—temptations which tear at the heart and rip out hope. Into this need for understanding, Jesus comes, above all else, wanting us to know that He does understand. His suffering has made Him the ultimate source to whom we can turn for understanding.

His suffering has made Him the ultimate source to whom we can turn for understanding.

Twice, Scripture refers to the fact that Christ is the "author" of our salvation: Hebrews 5:9 and 12:2. Both references address the fact that the actions by which He "wrote" were not accomplished by one quick stroke of a pen. The message He authors is not only one of forgiveness and eternal life being provided through His death, but added to this is His outline of a broader scope of salvation accomplished through His suffering. He introduces practical and powerful answers to life's tough times, bringing relief to the pressure points of our suffering.

It's as though the Scripture is saying, "The Savior not only saves you from sin, but He understands you as a person. He has come to provide the way through and out of your suffering, just as surely as He has provided a way for your release from sin and its power. So come to Jesus, the author of eternal salvation. Since He 'wrote the book,'

He understands every dimension and nuance of pain and suffering and has an answer to it all."

This idea of Christ as author of our salvation leads us to consider more deeply that His authoring has brought a complete salvation through death and suffering. It is a dual truth, profoundly described in the two passages in Hebrews that reveal Him as "author" in two different ways.

1. In Hebrews 5:9, the word *aitios* emphasizes His "causing" a complete salvation to be available to us.

2. In Hebrews 12:2, the word *archegos* underscores His "captaining" role.

In other words, He is an author who "causes" or brings into being and an author who "captains" or brings to completion. He leads us to full freedom through faith. He is both the launcher and the leader. He births a program of deliverance by His suffering, and He brings us through as He shares with us in our suffering.

But these facts do not solve the psychological dilemma most of us confront. The intellect probes and the emotions inquire, "How can He understand my suffering or really know what I feel?"

The first step in finding an answer to this is to avoid the mistake of confining Christ's sufferings to the cross.

We cannot diminish the reality of the fact that the cross involved deep and agonizing suffering. From the whipping post to the climax on Calvary, the record of Christ's death is one of horrible pain.

His beard was torn from His face. A crown of thorns was shoved into His head. Nails were pounded into His feet and hands. A spear split His side.

And in all of this, He refused to accept the sedative commonly given to those being crucified, choosing rather to tax pain to its limit. But no amount of suffering could destroy Him, not even the suffering that resulted in death.

Yet, as real as the pain and agony at Golgotha were, there is much more to understand about Christ's suffering for us—and with us. To understand how thoroughly His triumph extends into the details of our human experiences of stress and pain, we must look at more than Jesus' suffering and death. We must look at His life.

Jesus understands hunger. See Him in the wilderness after forty days of fasting, at the point when the human body begins to consume itself because it has used its own stored resources. See that man being urged to create loaves from stones to satisfy Himself and who refuses to do so. That man understands hunger.

Jesus understands thirst. The cry He makes from the cross comes from parched lips, dehydrated by extensive physical trauma. Jesus' "I thirst" is more than the appeal of a day laborer coming in from a scorching sun. This man had been burnt dry by the hate of cursing mockers, by the fires of divine judgment, and the drain of blood sacrifice. Jesus understands thirst.

Jesus understands weariness. A small ship is crossing Galilee. A storm's fury terrifies His companions, and Jesus sleeps. Strong men of experience who know the lake's many moods scream for help against the tempest's terror, yet the Visitor continues to sleep. His is not the sleep of the slothful or the lazy, or of one insensitive to the crisis at hand. His sleep, undisturbed by the buffeting and roar of the storm, is indicative of a man who is completely depleted by fatigue. His physical frame is worn; His stamina spent from ministering to multitudes. So worn and weary is He that even the splashing of the waves, the whipping of the boat, and the shrieking of the wind cannot awaken Him.

If you ever feel so tired you can't take another step, and if you wonder whether God knows that feeling, here's your answer: There is One who not only knows your weariness, but who says, "I'll walk the next step with you because I've been where you are—and further."

BUT THERE'S MORE THAN PHYSICAL STRESS TO LIFE'S sufferings. Consider the pain of being misunderstood, of being rejected, mocked, or unjustly accused. Consider the pain of being forgotten, of having people say you are evil for doing what you meant for good. Consider the pain of being unappreciated.

All of these pains are inflicted upon each of us. They are common to everyone. Some may bite their lip, tighten their grip, and stoically insist, "It's all right. I can take it." But no one really can. Not alone.

These things take an eventual toll on human nature. Unaided or untreated, the accumulation of such pain can provoke dour self-pity or produce arthritis of the soul. Sincere though our efforts at endurance may be, we can become whiners on the one hand or brittle on the other. Bracing ourselves against emotional pain without learning to receive the support of the only One who has mastered it by experience can only produce bitter fruit.

While saying, "It's all right," when it's really not, I can turn into something monstrous. And it won't be "all right" until I'm infused with the spirit of the One who truly knows what it is to be rejected, to be unrewarded, to have impossible demands

> *Bracing ourselves against emotional pain without learning to receive the support of the only One who has mastered it can only produce bitter fruit.*

imposed, to be surrounded by nit-picking critics who scrutinize every word and action, and hoping for a chance to find fault.

Dear one, the suffering Savior knows all this. He's been through it all. And He also knows man's inclination to feel that God doesn't really understand.

I began this chapter with a descriptive word picture. Allow me to conclude it with another one. It's called "God Leads a Pretty Sheltered Life."

Billions of people were scattered on a great plain before God's throne. Some of the groups near the front talked heatedly . . . not with cringing shame, but with belligerence.

"How can God judge us?" said one.

"What does He know about suffering?" snapped a brunette. She jerked back a sleeve to reveal a tattooed number from a Nazi concentration camp. "We endured terror, beatings, torture, death!"

In another group a black man lowered his collar. "What about this?" he demanded, showing an ugly rope burn. "Lynched for no crime but being black! We have suffocated in slave ships, been wrenched from loved ones, toiled till death gave release."

Far out across the plain were hundreds of such groups. Each had a complaint against God for the evil and suffering He permitted in His world. How lucky God was to live in Heaven where there was no weeping, no fear, no hunger, no hatred!

Indeed, what did God know about what man had been forced to endure in this world? "After all, God leads a pretty sheltered life," they said. So each group sent out a leader, chosen because he had suffered the most. There was a Jew, a black, an untouchable from India, an illegitimate, a person from Hiroshima, one from a Siberian gulag, and on it went.

In the center of the plain they consulted with each other. At last they were ready to present their case. It was rather simple: Before God would be qualified to be their judge, He must endure what they had endured. Their decision was that God "should be sentenced to live on Earth as a man!" But because He was God, they set certain safeguards to be sure He could not use His divine powers to help Himself:

Let Him be born a Jew.

Let the legitimacy of His birth be doubted, so that none would know who His Father was.

Let Him champion a cause so just, but so radical, that it brings down upon Him the hate, condemnation, and efforts of every major traditional and established religious authority to eliminate Him.

Let Him try to describe what no man has ever seen, felt, tasted, heard, or smelled . . . let Him try to communicate God to men.

Let Him be betrayed by His dearest friends.

Let Him be indicted on false charges, tried before a prejudiced jury, and convicted by a cowardly judge.

Let Him see what it is to be terribly alone and completely abandoned by every living thing.

Let Him be tortured and let Him die! Let Him die the most humiliating death, with common criminals.

As each leader announced his portion of the sentence, loud murmurs of approval went up from the great throngs of people.

But when the last had finished pronouncing sentence there was a long silence. No one uttered another word. No one moved. For suddenly all knew . . . God had already served His sentence. —Author unknown

Yes, the Visitor understands suffering and by reason of that understanding is not only fully accessible to our cry but fully able to give us release from the vicious power of suffering. He has absorbed it all in Himself, and Jesus now stands ready to dispense relief and recovery with His word of peace amidst your torment.

Heartache and mental anguish,
rip at the soul, men languish.
Hellish the sword now brandished,
piercing human minds.
Comes now the Lord of healing,
touched with our deepest feeling.
Truth from His lips is pealing,
freeing humankind.
Jesus, name above all names,
Savior, Healer, Understander
of the human predicament,
The Visitor.

BUT COULD HE BE TEMPTED?

6

From the time he was twelve years old, Californian Mark Wellman loved climbing mountains. As he grew older and more experienced, the athletic-looking outdoorsman took pride in having reached the summit of more than fifty Sierra Nevada peaks (as well as the French Alps). In 1982 following his twenty-second birthday, Mark reached the summit of the Seven Gables peak in the John Muir Wilderness. As he was making his descent, he fell one hundred feet and broke his lower back, resulting in paralysis from the waist down.

After months of therapy and recuperation, it became obvious to family and friends that the young climber's indomitable spirit had not been crushed. He was determined to stay active and find ways to do what he loved. Enrolling at a college in Saratoga, California, Mark earned a Park Management Certificate from West Valley College and worked as a park ranger in Yosemite National Park.

Being in the wilderness among the majestic mountains was therapeutic to Mark. Still, his longing to climb what he saw in the distance never dissipated. For a lifelong mountaineer, such a desire was a cruel temptation. Due to his paralysis, Mark could not climb on his own. His upper body strength was impressive, but he couldn't leverage himself without feeling in his legs.

While working in Yosemite, Mark met a climber by the name of Mike Corbett. Mike had scaled the legendary El Capitan forty-two times. He approached its granite face from every imaginable angle and was looking for a different way to take on the famous peak. As their friendship grew, Mark suggested that climbing El Capitan while rigged to a paraplegic would definitely be a way of ascending the mountain differently. What Mark could not accomplish on his own, he might be able to do supported by Mike. Even though no paraplegic had ever scaled it, the sheer granite face the height of three Empire State Buildings drew them like a magnet.

In July 1989, their months of preparation and conditioning were tested. The two began the assault with one goal in mind—reaching the top. Even though the rocks baked to 120 degrees every day, Mark maintained his focus by relying on Mike. For a man with only arms and no leg support, it meant 7,000 pull-ups, six inches at a time. Mike led and was the legs and other arms. On the seventh and final day of his climb, the headline of *The Fresno Bee* read, "Showing a Will of Granite." Accompanying the headline was a photo of Wellman being carried on the shoulders of his climbing companion Mike Corbett. A subtitle said, "Paraplegic and partner prove no wall is too high to scale." What many people did not know is that in order for Mark Wellman to pull himself up the face of the tallest, unbroken granite cliff in North America, his partner, Mike Corbett, had to climb it three times.

But Mark's climbing accomplishments didn't end there. Two years later, Wellman and Corbett set out to conquer Yosemite's other big wall, Half Dome. Thirteen days later, they reached the top of the 2,200 foot Half Dome. In July 1999, on the tenth anniversary of their historic climb, Mark and Mike made a repeat climb of El Capitan. Called "Return to the Challenge," they completed the climb in eleven days on a much more challenging route.

Mark Wellman has won the respect of able-bodied athletes. But he is a miraculous inspiration to those with special needs who battle overwhelming odds. Mark Wellman could not overcome his limitations alone though. There is no way he could have compensated for his condition; and without the ability, expertise, and willingness of someone like Mike Corbett, Mark Wellman would not be scaling mountains today. Mike's strength allows Mark to overcome his weaknesses.

In other words, what was impossible for one who had the experience but lacked the ability became a celebrated achievement when that one was teamed with another who had the experience and ability to compensate for them both.

In that enduring companionship is a picture of our relationship with Christ. Through His redemptive work on our behalf, the Divine Visitor is capable of coming to our aid and giving us the power to rise above seemingly insurmountable spiritual obstacles.

BUT WHAT DOES THE BIBLE MEAN IN HEBREWS 2:18 when it says Christ "suffered" temptation? I mean, after all, how can the quintessence of innocence and purity really be tempted?

But innocence means neither immunity nor invulnerability to sin, and purity means neither insensibility to nor incapability of sin. The mystery of the Incarnation, in which the divine and the human are fused into one, has caused many to wrestle with the question, "Could Jesus have sinned?"

This is a moot question now, because He didn't sin. Still, while it seems that His divine nature was not attracted by sin's power, His true humanity held the capability of sensing sin and needing to choose a response to it. Christ's absolute sinlessness would not have weakened the force and pain of temptation; it would have intensified it.

Though sinless in Himself, Jesus suffered the presence of sin around him.

For example, a person from outside who walks into a coal mine while wearing a white linen suit is obviously more vulnerable and sensitive to the dusty environment than those who are already blackened by their toil there. So it was with Jesus when He plunged into the mineshaft of this world's sin. Though sinless in Himself, He suffered the presence of sin around Him. In the midst of this, the painful pressure of evil was set against Him, taunting Him, saying, "Act now. Do anything You want." Christ suffered temptation.

Yet the even greater reality of Jesus' victory over sin's pressure and temptation is that, while clothed in perfect purity and walking through the inky mire of all that provokes and produces human sinning, Christ continually embraces the sinful. He regularly draws them to Himself and, amazingly, leaves each one imprinted with

His holiness while He remains untarnished by sin's stain or power. No, loved ones, innocence is not immunity.

PREPARING FOR A RECENT TRIP TO AFRICA, THE LAW required that I be vaccinated against several diseases common to the area of my intended visit. As with all such injections, I was given a vaccine containing the very viruses to which I would be vulnerable. Germs were literally put into my arm—some cholera, some typhoid, a small colony of each. Thus immunized, my body was able to form a resistance against the full force of these potentially fatal diseases.

But Jesus was not immunized against sin. He was not inoculated with "just a little" to brace His pure system against the shock of the world's sin and evil. Instead, because there was no sin in Him, his vulnerability to it and all of its ravages was so much greater.

It is difficult for us to appreciate the magnitude of our sins. Since none of mankind had experienced sinlessness, we cannot understand the full force of Christ's suffering in sin's presence. We may, on occasion, be repulsed by sin— sins of the grotesque or gross level. But the sting of sin's slightest presence is below our threshold of pain. We need to seek an understanding of Jesus' suffering of this sting.

We miss the mark if we make the mistake of supposing that His sinless life was a "no contest" match making Him invulnerable to His opponent or somehow desensitized to sin's clawing efforts at entry into His pure nature. Jesus was tempted by the burning pressure of sin as it pressed on in its infectious quest to poison this Visitor from another realm. The fact that He was "in all points tempted as we are, yet without sin" (Hebrews 4:15) constitutes a dimension of suffering far beyond our comprehension. The presence and power of sin has been felt far more by this untarnished Visitor; this One who never knew the pollution of Earth's sooted, mine-like atmosphere. He has experienced it far more than we can ever grasp.

Now consider the sufferer's Savior. There is another dimension of Christ's suffering that we would do well to study more carefully—that He suffered for us. First Peter 4:1–2 says this explicitly: Just as Christ dying has accomplished a dual provision for us, so has His suffering. Every aspect of His redemptive work is rich with wealth for our resource.

Most of us readily understand how Jesus, in dying, paid the price of our sin and provided the gifts of life and forgiveness. But few realize that His suffering was more than merely a preliminary to His death. Jesus' suffering was redemptive too. His suffering was substitutionary. He suffered in our stead, absorbing in Himself the horrible implications of sin's impact on the human frame.

The Rotherham translation, though clumsy in its technical rendition of the Hebrew text of Isaiah 53:4–5, nonetheless conveys the biblical truth with power.

> Yet surely our sicknesses, he, carried, And as for our pains, he bare the burden of them, —But, we, accounted him stricken. Smitten of God and humbled, Yet, he, was pierced for transgressions that were ours, was crushed for iniquities that were ours, —the chastisement for our well-being, was upon Him, And by his stripes, there is healing for us.

Jesus' suffering holds a provision for our healing. Feel the fact and the force of that truth. The preceding passage from Isaiah, joined to Matthew 8:17 and 1 Peter 2:24, shows how completely biblical it is to reach out to the Lord Jesus Christ for deliverance from suffering and sickness just as surely as we can reach to Him for salvation from our sins.

Paul reminded early believers that their forgetfulness of the provision of the cross was even causing some to experience a premature death (1 Corinthians 11:24–30).

His reminder of the valid and powerful participation in the Lord's Table called attention to this fact. "For some of you," He seems to say, "in violating the appropriate participation in the Lord's Table, have experienced an early death."

Along with these reminders from the Word of God, hear the Holy Spirit speaking from Psalm 103:2–3: "And forget not all His benefits; Who forgives all your iniquities, Who heals all your diseases."

There is no question about the dimension of His promise. But there have been real questions at times with my own faith. Perhaps you, like I, find it easier to believe and receive forgiveness for sins than to believe and receive healing for our bodies. Why that should be the case is beyond me, for it is clear that the greater miracle is the forgiveness of sin. It is a much greater problem than sickness.

It is a marvelously joyous and precious thing to testify to the times we call upon the Lord for healing and experience it. But what about the times when faith seems weak, when healing seems remote? This is not because God is taunting or loveless, but because healing faith seems to elude us. At such points we tend to resign to either philosophy or bitterness: on the one hand, we rationalize the situation as "God's will" or we become angry and say He doesn't care. But Jesus Christ our Savior in going all the way through His sufferings has provided a better alternative.

Remember how Mike Corbett scaled El Capitan three times in order to make it possible for Mark Wellman to maneuver the granite face of that mountain just once? In that human illustration lies a prophetic glimpse of a divine principle.

Dear one, there is a force, a power, in Jesus' suffering; a power to break the ability of pain, injury, or sorrow to dominate you, even when these things seem to persist beyond prayer. Hebrews 2:18 states, "Since he himself has gone through suffering and temptation, he is able to help us when we are being tempted" (NLT). Christ's suffering has the power to absorb the most hellish or human attack, the most tragic or traumatic pain, or whatever it is that seems to exceed your capacity to endure.

Without Jesus, suffering can grind people down until they're reduced to emotional pulp; forced to surrender or driven to nervous exhaustion or breakdown. Suffering can so debilitate resistance that we finally concede to sin—not because of lust,

> *Without Jesus, suffering can grind people down until they're reduced to emotional pulp.*

unbelief, or rebellion, but simply because of weariness in the battle. But the transforming, revitalizing truth is that in His suffering, the Savior has penetrated the eye of the storm. He has shattered the power of suffering to destroy us.

Jesus has broken suffering's ability to reduce us to bitterness, faithlessness, or disobedience. Hear Him whisper, "I want to fill you with the same life that brought Me through suffering; that kept Me from shrinking before the fires of hell's worst workings; that kept Me from wearying in well doing and from becoming bitter or turning to animosity. When I was unthanked, I didn't retaliate. When people rejected Me, I didn't withdraw. My availability to love and serve them is yours."

And Jesus is saying this that we might take it—to receive that part of our salvation that was purchased by His suffering for us. First, hear the Savior say, "Come to Me, I understand." Then hear Him add, "I will penetrate your suffering with My life, and not only will you survive, you will be victorious in the midst of it all."

THERE IS ONE MORE FACET OF TRUTH I WANT TO share with you: The Savior's sufferers extend our meditation on Jesus' suffering for us, and it is His call to people who will suffer with Him.

Now this may seem a peculiar focus, since our primary point has been to see His provision for our deliverance from and victory through suffering. But we will miss a treasured truth if we overlook God's purpose for each of us in the suffering we have experienced. Even as He, having suffered, understands us, so He longs to minister to others through His people who have shared in His victory in the midst of their own pain. Just as the free gift of salvation is ministered to mankind by those who have received forgiveness and life in Christ, so the joy of victory over the power of suffering is given to others by those of us who have experienced His sustaining power: "That we may be able to comfort those who are in any trouble with the comfort with which we ourselves are comforted by God," Paul said to the Corinthians (2 Corinthians 1:4).

Jesus is looking for people who will minister His life, His truth, and His love to other sufferers and do it in the same spirit that He ministers to us. He is always patient with the suffering. He comes offering full healing and complete deliverance, but somehow many of His own are unable to receive everything He is willing to give. Weakness, fear, pride, spiritual blindness, doubt, or ignorance of the Word all have something to do with this. And yet, the perfect Savior who suffered for us is perfectly patient with me, with you, with any who fail to grasp all that He has for them. And He calls us to be that way with one another. He points the way for us to partner with others in their suffering in the same way. He has met us with understanding and grace and without criticism. In the Savior's call for sufferers to minister to the suffering, light is shed for us on some otherwise misunderstood passages in the Bible.

Romans 8:16–17 says, "The Spirit Himself bears witness with our spirit that we are children of God, and if children, then heirs—heirs of God and joint heirs with Christ . . ." We believe and love that part. But it adds, ". . . if indeed we suffer with Him, that we may also be glorified together."

Philippians 1:29 says, "For to you it has been granted on behalf of Christ, not only to believe in Him, but also to suffer for His sake."

Philippians 3:10 says, "That I may know Him . . . and the fellowship of His sufferings."

Many simply overlook or explain away such verses. Still others make them a case for sickness and misery as though that were prerequisite to righteousness, as though God willed people to suffer. This train of thought can breed self-pitying, whimpering saints who lament, "God must want me to go through this suffering, oh me! It is the cross He wants me to bear." But that isn't what these verses teach. To either deny or twist them in order to pretend there are no suffering saints or to strain them to frame a doctrine of "God wills my suffering" is to miss the point on both sides.

In all of this, you see, Jesus is speaking to us, saying, "I have shown understanding of your suffering and by My presence I have taught you that I can transform into victory the anguish, the pain, the burden, the pressure, and the inclination to give up. But child, I offer you a partnership in an even greater victory—a triumph that exceeds any joy you've ever tasted."

And patiently He begins to teach us.

"Child, there are many you will touch who don't know the release, deliverance, and victory I have for them. These include My own as well as others yet to enter the kingdom. I am asking you not to try to persuade them of truth but to demonstrate its power in love. Suffer with them patiently and with understanding.

"Their heads hang and their hearts droop with despair. They are overcome by burdens that are more than they know how to handle. They have not as yet learned the availability of My life power in the midst of their suffering. Your words will not help them now, only your love.

"I have taught you of My presence and victory that you might answer this call. Will you go in My name and stand beside them? As I have come to you in your suffering, will you go now and suffer with them?

"Weep with those who weep. Be with those who are bound as though you also are bound. Lift up their feeble hands. Comfort their troubled minds. Bear one another's burdens and fulfill My law. As the Father sent Me, even in suffering, to open the door of release, so send I you."

Have you ever sat with someone as they have spilled out the pain and hurt of disappointment, failure, or tragedy? Have you learned how they need much more than hurried, pretentious, all-knowing counsel? Job's comforters still plague the afflicted with their self-righteous attitude of "Now, here's what you need to do about that." But the parroting of Bible texts and theological truths is not their greatest need at the moment.

Of course, people to whom we minister need the Word of God. And it will penetrate the deepest part of their being and bring comfort, hope, and correction. But the Word of God needs to be ministered in the love of God sensitively and in the spirit of gentle counsel. The Word must be given as the incarnate Word. The truth as it has been made flesh in you, revealed by your coming, your visiting, your loving. And the best way for this to occur is when a sensible, sensitive soul comes to sit beside a sufferer and say, "Listen, I understand. I feel your pain and I'm going to stand with you through it. I don't have all the answers but I am with you in the name of He who does. And until we find His way through this, I'm here to suffer with you."

One of my most moving experiences was when a well-known man poured out to me the story of his moral failure and his dishonesty in business. It was painful for him but he held nothing back. His contrition was real and his repentance deep. But when the conversation was nearly over, I turned to face him squarely, and I said, "Brother, no matter what happens, no matter what is brought against you because of your failure, I make this commitment to you: I will stand by you on any terms, not only personally, but also in public—not to affirm your guiltlessness, but to affirm my support to you as a brother in Christ."

I saw a strong and dynamic man reduced to tears. He took my hand as he said, "You've given me the greatest gift that anyone could possibly give me."

It is to such people that Jesus calls us, dear friend. We are not called just to know that He understands, that He has penetrated the core of the things that torment mankind, and that He's broken the power of suffering. He doesn't want us to know that just suffering can no longer reduce us to something less than God intends us to be. But now He is saying, "I want you to bring others to know these things as well. And I want you to love them, realizing that loving them will often require you to suffer with them patiently even as My loving you has required that of Me."

IT IS A FULL CIRCLE, DEAR FRIEND. BE HEALED IN YOUR suffering. Be released from your suffering. Both are provided in our salvation—His work for us. Receive your wholeness, and then go—and be healing balm to a suffering world.

HIS WOUNDS

7

When Merrill Womach traipsed the halls of Northwest Bible College in the forties, he was every co-ed's heartthrob. His dark brown wavy hair framed a face that more often than not boasted a million dollar smile. But Merrill's good looks were not his most envied attribute. Merrill had an amazing tenor voice. As he sang in chapel, those around him knew he'd been blessed with a God-given talent. Much like the well-known Italian virtuoso Mario Lanza, Merrill had a range that seemingly wouldn't quit.

Following school, Merrill married his college sweetheart and went on to start a music company, supplying businesses with recorded music. He also established himself as a Christian singer and performed sacred concerts in churches across the country. Because he had obtained a private pilot's license, Merrill often flew himself between clients and concerts. He sat in the cockpit looking beyond the control panel to the breathtaking scenery below, singing directly to the Lord in full voice.

In November 1961 while flying from San Diego to Spokane, the plane developed mechanical problems over southern Oregon. Merrill did his best to make an emergency landing, but the wings of the small aircraft clipped a grove of trees in the wooded area where the plane lost altitude. An enormous explosion followed. The plane burst into flames. Having survived the crash and explosion, Merrill, temporarily blinded and severely burned, proceeded to stumble through the woods in search of help. Listening for the sound of cars on the highway, he collapsed on the side of the road waiting for help to arrive.

When some passersby stopped to help, they carefully placed Merrill in the backseat of their car and drove to the nearest hospital in Klamath Falls. Amazingly, Merrill sang hymns until they reached the emergency room. Once there, doctors attended to the man without any recognizable facial features. His once handsome face was now charred, blackened, and swollen. Doctors also found that his synthetic wool sports coat had become hardened like a metal jacket from the intense heat. (Curiously, for some reason he can't explain to this day, Merrill had not removed his sports coat prior to take-off as was his custom.) The plaster-like material had served to protect Merrill's upper body from burns and guaranteed healthy skin tissue that would be used in subsequent grafts.

In the months that followed, Merrill found that despite his disfigurement, his voice had actually become stronger. He continued singing for churches as well as schools, conventions, and service clubs. Frequently he would visit people in hospitals and convalescent homes. Patients who were terminally ill or deeply depressed would welcome his visits. Merrill was capable of touching the deep pain in their lives. He discovered that what he had suffered as a result of the accident was actually a means of ministry. Those with emotional and physical wounds were encouraged to be in the presence of someone who had found the ability to rise above tragedy and experience God's healing peace.

Although the wounds of physical disfigurement are a far cry from the wounds our Savior bore on our behalf, Merrill Womach's scarred face does give us a slight view of the role the Divine Visitor's wounds play in our lives. It is

It is more than scar tissue that points to our redemption. It is a badge of identity that allows the Divine Visitor's entrance into the Father's presence.

more than scar tissue that points to our redemption. It is a badge of identity that allows His entrance into the Father's presence where He can freely intercede on behalf of wounded and flawed followers. Through Merrill's wounds, countless individuals have been nudged nearer to the Great Physician.

ALL TOO FREQUENTLY, CHRIST'S SUFFERINGS AND HIS wounds are seen as one and the same. Yet each is a specific expenditure within redemption's full purchasing price. Each feature of the Visitor's experience secures a potential for our triumph over the effects of specific issues in life that we could never overcome through our own efforts. That is what Hebrews 10:1 really means: The law (our own efforts) can never make those who approach God perfect or complete. The following verses of the text explain why that is true.

The Old Testament Scriptures foreshadowed many of the features of Christ's impending fulfillment of God's plan for salvation. One detail after another, through a dim foretaste or a shadow as the words occurred, was shown forth.

For example, Jesus was foreshadowed as the Lamb of God (John 1:29). First, slain before the foundation of the world (1 Peter 1:20), and second, sent to take away the sin of the world (John 1:29). In that foreshadowing, the sacrificial lamb of the Old Testament forecast the substitutionary death of Christ, the Lamb of God given to be the covering for our sins. Now in remarkable detail, a silhouetted forecast of the coming of the Savior was shown in the Levitical system (Deuteronomy 16:1–8). But there was one thing that the Old Testament's sacrificial lamb did not foreshadow: the wounded Christ.

As pointed out earlier in this book, when sacrificed according to Moses' directive, lambs were killed quickly, mercifully, in a moment. Not only was a lamb not wounded, but to qualify for sacrificial purposes each animal had to be bruise- and blemish-free. Interestingly enough, the very perfection that God required of a sacrificial animal to foreshadow the perfect sacrifice He would eventually provide, disallowed a wounded creature being used for the Old Testament sacrifices. Yet while the wounds of Christ were not foreshadowed in the Old Testament type, they were foretold by the prophets.

The pathway of understanding begins with the quotation of Psalm 40:6–8 regarding our study of Hebrews 10:5–7:

> "Sacrifice and offering You did not desire; My ears You have opened. Burnt offering and sin offering You did not require. Then I said, 'Behold I come; In the scroll of the

book it is written of Me. I delight to do Your will, O my
God, And Your law is within my heart.'"

These words are taken from a passage which scholars
agree predicted the coming of the Messiah. But we are
given history as well as prophecy, for we are expressly
informed that when the Son of God left the glory world to
enter this one, He spoke these words recorded in Psalm 40
by David a thousand years before Christ.

In light of those facts, might we ask, "When did Jesus
Christ actually say these words? Recorded by David a thousand years before Christ, when were they spoken?" The
answer is only clear if we see the setting—an actual conversation between the Son, Second Person of the Trinity, and
the Father, First Person of the Trinity, just as Jesus was
preparing to leave the Father's throne to come to earth. Let
your thoughts fly with mine to a scene in the eternal past; a
scene which occurs in the very throne room of highest glory.

Only a few places in the Bible give a glimpse of heaven.
Ezekiel 40 describes the prophet's vision of God's glory, and
Isaiah 6 describes the prophet's sense of being ushered
before God's throne. Perhaps the most panoramic scene of
the throne is drawn by John as he records his vision of the
throng at worship in the book of Revelation (chapter 4).
These scenes project a throne room so enormous, so expan-
sive that it has a virtual lake, a "crystal sea" as it is called, in
front of God's throne. Here, innumerable hosts worship as

praise echoes through the halls of this arenalike cathedral, the enormity of which staggers our imaginations.

The Bible hardly gives us a complete picture of the Godhead—the Trinity—enthroned. Who can imagine it? But what we do know is that the Son of God is seated on the right hand of the Father. He was there before all worlds, long before becoming flesh to dwell among us, always having been ever present with the Father and the Spirit.

And can you imagine that here, in the splendor of this throne room, a moment occurred, one that the Bible speaks of as an instant in the timelessness of eternity past? The Father, the Son, and the Holy Spirit took counsel together concerning the projected plan of man's creation—a plan requiring the provision of a redeemer. It was here, on His own initiation that the Son agreed to be that redeemer; agreed that, when need dictated and the Father directed, He would go to mankind's rescue.

Now the decision has been inscribed in the annals of eternity. It would be much later that this will be announced by the prophet, Isaiah, and written in the Father's book on earth: "For unto us a Child is born, Unto us a Son is given" (Isaiah 9:6). Thus, we gain a glimpse into why it is that the Bible says, "Before the foundation of the world, the Lamb of God was slain" (1 Peter 1:19–21, paraphrased).

Let such a scene provoke thankful praise. Before time as we know it began, man's salvation was considered and planned in the council chambers of heaven.

BUT NOW, IN OUR IMAGINATIONS, MOVING OUT beyond that juncture into eternity, we step into time and begin to trek the centuries which tabulate the cavalcade of man's history. We reach a point in which time's passage has long been in progress. Creation, the flood, Babel, and Abraham are far behind. We have moved past Israel's Egyptian bondage, their deliverance, and the passage of the Red Sea. The Ten Commandments have been given. The wilderness journey is behind. The Promised Land has been fought for and taken. Israel's and Judah's kings have come and gone, as has the Babylonian captivity, and the return of the remnant from exile.

And we enter the silent period where prophetic voices seem stilled. A holy hush has enveloped the heavenlies as all creation anticipates the coming fulfillment of generations of divinely inspired prophecy.

And then it happens. The fullness of time has come and the Father is ready to send forth His Son. And it is precisely then that He turns to His Son, and on the basis of an agreement made ages ago, He simply says, "Now."

They gaze at one another momentarily as both Father and Son knowingly weigh the moment and its cost. Then, without hesitation, in a gesture containing actions and implications beyond our grasp, the Son lays aside garments of glory and turns to the Father with these words: "You were not satisfied with animal sacrifices, slain and burnt before You as offerings for sin. See, I have come to do Your will, to lay down My life, just as the Scriptures said that I would. Sacrifice and offerings You did not desire. But a body You have prepared for Me and burnt offerings and sacrifices for sin You had no pleasure." Then He says, "Behold I have come. In the volume of the book it is written of Me to do Your will, O God."

Do you capture it? It had been written in the volume of heaven before all worlds; prophesied on earth hundreds of years before, and now the moment had come.

Can we fathom all that really happened in that moment? In that miracle of miracles? Jesus' preincarnate glory was not in the kind of body we're used to seeing. We cannot imagine His form. This is not to suggest that He had some bizarre, extraterrestrial frame, but simply to assert, as the epistle to the Philippians says, that He was then "in the form of God" (2:6). Yet He lays aside whatever that form expresses in its eternal splendor and willingly takes on human form—the physical expression of man, the creature. "It has been written in the volume of the book and now I go, to take on that body You have readied for Me," He says.

But at that moment, loved one, that body is hardly a body at all. It is but a cell in the womb of a virgin, in a small city of a tiny nation, in one small corner of a fallen planet.

And in one microsecond, the primal form of the Son disappears from the throne of heaven and in that same split moment, the Holy Spirit of God has placed the life of the Second Person of the Godhead within the womb of a maiden.

The inconceivable has been conceived.

The Word will become flesh.

God will live and breathe among us.

And in coming to take that body, He knows full well that unlike the sacrificial lamb foreshadowing Him, He will be wounded. Merrill Womach had no idea that as his plane took off that Thanksgiving morning his handsome face would be burned beyond recognition. He hadn't a clue that in the weeks and years to follow, his monster-like countenance would evoke mocking and terror. Only the years would erase his emotional pain as he saw how his scars allowed his entrance into the lives of other emotionally and physically scarred people. But Jesus knew, in advance, the wounds He would be forced to endure once He entered our sphere.

Jesus knew, in advance, the wounds He would be forced to endure once He entered our sphere.

The Book which said, "A body will be prepared" (Hebrews 10:5) has also written into it additional provisional clauses. Salvation will require the sacrifice to be indelibly wounded with marks that will tell eternally of the fact that a divine visit was made. And in His coming, He is consenting to every word: "to do Your will, O God" (10:7). Isaiah says, "He was wounded for our transgressions, He was bruised for our iniquities" (53:5), and He who is taking on this body which You have prepared to fulfill those words knows what they mean. "Wound" means broken flesh; "bruise" means a beaten body.

Jesus knew that the body He would take on earth would be wounded, bruised, beaten, battered, slapped, and have the face hairs pulled out. Isaiah had spoken of Him: "I gave My back to those who struck Me, And My cheeks to those who plucked out the beard" (50:6). He would also be beaten for our peace, the whippings would leave stripes that would be an agency for mankind's healing.

Other prophetic statements awaited confirmation by His coming for wounding. Read Psalm 22:16:

> For dogs have surrounded Me; The congregation of the wicked has enclosed Me. They pierced My hands and My feet.

Zechariah spoke:

> And I will pour on the house of David and on the inhab-itants of Jerusalem the Spirit of grace and supplication; then they will look on Me whom they have pierced. Yes,

they will mourn for Him as one mourns for his only son,
and grieve for Him as one grieves for a firstborn (12:10).

Climactically, Isaiah 52:14 puts it this way: "So His visage was marred more than any man."

Franz Delitzsch, the renowned Old Testament and Hebrew language scholar, unfolds the force of the expression used in the Isaiah reference, explaining the language here conveys a prophecy of a person being so distorted that all likeness to a man is destroyed—complete disfigurement, until all that remains is a grotesque, battered hulk.

So it is that the fact of His wounding was only revealed through the words of the prophets, for no animal type could reveal it. Through prophetic lips and pens, the Holy Spirit declared that Jesus would come, not only as a bleeding, dying lamb but as a suffering and wounded man. And when Christ, our Savior, just prior to His entry into this world, said, "Behold, I have come to do Your will, O God" (Hebrews 10:9), He fully understood the implication of the words. He would be required to fulfill all the revealed, prophesied, written will of God.

And the Visitor came to bear those wounds.

HIS BLOOD

8

*F*or Mark Thallander, the summer of 2003 was (in the words of Charles Dickens) the best of times and the worst of times. This world-class organist from Southern California accomplished what most church musicians only dream about. He played the organ for the Beethoven *Mass in C* and the Haydn *Te Deum* at Carnegie Hall. In addition, he was privileged to perform at St. Patrick's Cathedral in New York City and present a lecture for the national convention of the Royal Canadian College of Organists at the National Library in Ottawa. If that weren't enough, he'd been asked to play in Washington, D.C. at the national convention of one of the fastest growing evangelical denominations.

From the nation's capital, Mark flew to Maine to spend some free time with a friend and play at a church in Worcester, Massachusetts. That's when tragedy struck.

Following the morning worship service, he drove through the beautiful New England countryside, headed toward his friend's cottage. He could barely see the road through the windshield, as a horrendous thunderstorm refused to let up. Exiting the turnpike, his car began to hydroplane. Before he could slow, it spun out of control. The Toyota 4Runner flew into a ditch before hitting the guardrail and flipping over into oncoming traffic.

The SUV was demolished. Mark's left arm was torn out of its socket and crushed in at least three places. Even though his glasses were thrown off, he could tell by looking at the windshield, blanketed in a red mist, that he'd lost a lot of blood.

Within a few minutes the paramedics arrived and rushed him to the nearest hospital—forty miles away. The reason he'd seen so much red liquid splattered in the wreckage was soon called to his attention. He'd lost nearly 70 percent of his total blood supply. The doctors didn't mince words. With that amount of blood loss, his condition was extremely critical. The doctors confronted him with both good news and bad news.

The good news was the near certainty that his life could be spared. The bad news was the cost of saving his life. They'd have to amputate his left arm.

Believing his career as an organist depended on having both arms, the news left Mark depressed but depending on God's arms. He was too weak to offer any resistance. He prayed for the Lord's will to be done.

Following the amputation, Mark looked over at the limp sleeve of his hospital gown. *God was the One who had given me my love of music and my ability to play,* he thought to himself. *Could this really be part of God's plan for my life?* Mark wondered if he'd ever be able to play the organ again.

As cards and letters began to arrive in the hospital, Mark began to visualize something beautiful emerging from something so ugly. He began to picture himself playing the organ again. That dream took place just three months later when he played an organ duet for his dad's memorial service. Although he could only use his right hand, his recovery had begun (both physically and emotionally).

Over the next several months, Mark was humbled by the way family, friends, and church members reached out to him. Thanks to their financial support, funds were supplied to pay his uninsured medical bills. They also raised monies to provide Mark with two prosthetic left arms and three removable hands. The fingers on one of them are spaced so that he can play two notes on the organ with it. His fear of losing his profession never came to be.

As Mark sits at the organ and plays the great old hymns of the church in a new way, he is mindful of God's provision in his life. As the sanctuary fills with melodies of faith that refer to the blood of Christ, Mark is aware like never before that life is dependent on the blood—both physically as well as spiritually.

Now, imagine losing 70 percent of your blood. Although Mark may not have known how critical his situation was at the time, given the presence of blood everywhere, he could have guessed. You can't live without having a certain quantity of blood in your body. And spiritually speaking, you can't live without having a certain Visitor's blood flowing in and through you.

IT IS COMMON IN THE WRITINGS OF MOST HYMN writers, poets, and theological authors to capitalize the word "blood" when referring to the blood of Jesus. This has been done traditionally because they are well aware it is a substance of tremendous significance. For my own part, I wish this tradition still continued to this day. For we live in a day when we would do well to increase our sensitivity to the place of the blood of Christ. In it, we touch the heart of God's redemptive plan.

There is an awesome responsibility on the part of believers to understand the importance of Jesus' blood. The fact that almost everyone is emotionally affected by the sight or thought of blood is of no small significance.

We shudder to think of taking a life, and there is a deep-seated reaction with regard to bloodshed. We sense its essential part in our physical survival and often are repulsed simply by the sight of blood.

When God becomes involved, we know there is something that cannot be dismissed lightly from thought. He becomes very serious about a program of rescue—one that demands blood. God deals with the matter head on. Hebrews 9:22 says "Without shedding of blood there is no remission."

Why? Our human sensitivities cry for an answer.

Fourteen hundred years before Christ (over 3,400 years ago), the Lord spoke saying,

> For the life of the flesh is in the blood, and I have given it to you upon the altar to make atonement for your souls; for it is the blood that makes atonement for the soul (Leviticus 17:11).

In these words, God explicitly says that the atonement for man's sin, the reconciliation, was at the price of blood, and that He was giving that payment to man. But He also makes a categorical statement about man's life: "The life of the flesh is in the blood." That fact was penned by Moses about 1440 BC. Since then, the physiological truth of that scriptural statement has been proven time and again.

The function and survival of the human body depend on blood. Indeed, the body's essence is wrapped up in it, although science has only lately verified that fact. Over three millennia ago, God was seeking to draw man's attention to the blood's significance: "For it is the life of all flesh. Its blood sustains its life" (Leviticus 17:14). And it is that substance, that essence of our existence that forms the foundation for securing the salvation of the human race.

THUS, GOD BREATHED THE BREATH OF LIFE INTO Adam. And every living creature enjoys life in that same way. Once birth has occurred, breathing must begin, for life comes to us one breath at a time. And when it comes, it is rushed to every cell by the blood that courses through the veins. Yet oddly enough, that river which carries life stops when its precious cargo (oxygen) is stopped. So it should come as no surprise that blood is at the heart of redemption's program, for it is the very center of life.

The theme of the blood of Christ will occupy the endless ages of eternity.

And at the heart of it all, God found it necessary for Himself, the Creator, to partake of flesh and blood. He knew He had to show us how to live life to its fullest and to pour Himself out as a sacrifice for our death-deserving twistedness, and then look into the future. The theme of the blood of Christ will occupy the endless ages of eternity.

Referring to the redeemed as they gather around the throne of God, Revelation 5:9–10 says,

> And they sang a new song saying: 'You are worthy to take the scroll, And to open its seals; For You were slain, And have redeemed us to God by Your blood Out of every tribe and tongue and people and nation, And have made us kings and priests to our God.'

It is clear in this passage that voluntary praise for the blood of Christ will fill eternity. Knowing what we do of God's ways and nature, we can safely conclude that the eternal song will continue for a definite reason. God did not bring us to that point to be chanting robots. But we will forever be gaining insight into the wisdom of God's way of restoration through the blood of the Lamb.

Loved one, if the passing eons will increase our gratitude, how wise would we be to consider how much our present life can be enhanced by prayerful, thoughtful meditation on the blood of Jesus?

As you can see, this is no casual theme. We are at the very heart of all physical life and at the core of all human salvation. It is little wonder then that it is the basis of eternal praise.

THERE IS SOMETHING OF A MYSTERY ABOUT THE blood. As it is revealed in the Scripture, the Bible says it "speaks" (Hebrews 12:24). We are first introduced to this phenomenon in the book of Genesis.

Cain has killed Abel, his brother, and the Lord has come to challenge him on the issue of the murder.

"Where is Abel, your brother?" God inquires.

Cain answers, "How should I know? Am I supposed to keep track of him wherever he goes?"

And then the Lord makes this telling statement: "The voice of your brother's blood cries out to Me from the ground" (Genesis 4:9–10, paraphrased).

With these words we are given this revelation: Blood transcends the physical realm in its influence and significance.

Further evidence of the supra-physical qualities of blood is seen in God's instructions to the Israelites. Among the ordinances given when they prepared to occupy Canaan was the Lord's direction that if a body was found slain in an open field and the murderer be untraced, a sacrifice must be offered by the residents of the nearest city. Otherwise the defilement of guilt for the blood that was violently shed there fell on the people of that community. Such was the power of the presence and witness of blood. In a similar context, God spoke concerning the sin, bloodshed, and violence of Sodom and Gomorrah: "I will go down and see whether these reports are true or not. Then I will know" (Genesis 18:21, paraphrased). Bloodshed bears a testimony of its own then.

The force of this concept comes to bear on us with reference to the blood of Christ. In Hebrews 12:24, we are told to consider, since the blood of Abel bore a testimony, how much more the blood of Christ speaks better things for us.

The point is clear. Just as Abel's blood cried for God's justice where injustice had been committed, Jesus' blood also cries out for God's action. But His blood is not calling for justice to be done; rather it is declaring that justice has been accomplished. And it is because of that power of the blood to bear witness that Jesus' first words from Calvary, spoken just as His blood began to pour from His body, were, "Father, forgive them" (Luke 23:34). The message He sounded forth then continues to work forgiveness now.

This fact is underscored in Hebrews 11:4. The present tense verb form of "speaks" emphasizes the present ongoing action. Jesus' blood is still speaking.

There is a continuous testimony still being borne to the excellence and the power of and effectiveness for cleansing by the blood that was spilled on a Judean hillside centuries ago.

With the theme of the blood, we enter enormous dimensions of truth. There is a splendor here, something beautiful, glorious, and unfathomable in the blood of

Christ. It is not a morbid study but a positive, powerful, and dynamic one. God's Word unveils the meaning of the blood of Christ from three perspectives: as a tradition, a transaction, and a transfusion.

IN THE NINTH CHAPTER OF HEBREWS, THE SACRIFICES offered by the Old Testament priests are shown to be symbolic, although the opening words note that the Old Testament ordinances concerning blood sacrifices had specific ritual patterns that needed to be literally observed. In their symbolism, these ordinances were something like a painting. It was God's way, through traditional observances, to introduce His people to what He was preparing them for in the future. It is important for us to understand that these laws and ordinances were not an end in themselves. David understood that long before the coming of Christ. In Psalm 51:16–17, he says, "Sacrifice and offering are not what you are seeking in the long run, O God" (paraphrased).

The New Testament teaches us that the Old Testament ordinances were given as a schoolmaster; a tutor to help bring us to Christ in the same way a child is trained until he can come into his own full potential.

So the law of the sacrifices was a schoolroom for mankind, intending to bring him, to bring us, to God's highest and best. As with any early schooling, the goal is not the student's recitation of the alphabet but his learning to arrange those letters into words and read them with understanding. He isn't expected just to learn the multiplication tables, but he is taught so that he may gain the ability to solve mathematical problems. And so it was with the Old Testament traditions. God was, in essence, teaching ABC's and multiplication tables so that by these lessons, we would later be able to understand His plan and purpose in the Redeemer He would send and in the redemption He would provide.

Against the backdrop of the legal traditions of the Law of Moses, life and death can be discerned. From the ABC's of tradition, we can discover the One who is the Word. And in reading of Him, we learn the mathematics of life's meaning. He is the sum of all and the focus of the letters of the Law. Everything adds up in Him, and life's purposes multiply when we learn to solve our problems through Christ so that traditions and symbols have a purpose. In the midst of them all, God was teaching preliminary lessons for the more advanced teachings mankind would need to learn.

THE FIRST LESSON WE WOULD NEED TO LEARN IS THAT sin is serious. Through the traditions of the Law it became clear: Sin cannot go unremitted; unpaid for. Payment must be exacted for all sins committed.

The mindset of our world observes sin casually, as a sort of sorry trait of the race, and the less said about it the better. "You know how things are," someone says with a shrug. "It's too bad; just let it go." Most of us agree it's unfortunate that people are thoughtless and unkind, that tempers fly and violent events occur, that trust is violated and integrity compromised. "But what can you do? It's human nature," one says. And with that, as though sin were a mere whimsy, the issue of sin—its root and its fruit—is philosophically dispensed with, and the world emits a sigh of hopeless indifference as its deepest sign of regret—if any regret is registered at all.

This spirit must be confronted or it will too readily dilute our understanding. True human freedom will never evolve from rationalizing our sin, and this casual view must be identified and uprooted wherever it may have seeped into the mindset of many believers.

But many who receive Christ carry into their new life the empty theology of their surrounding culture. And unless this vacuum of pop theology is filled with truth, empty ideas will produce barren hearts, which lead to hollow living.

So we must ask: How does the Bible view sin? The Bible teaches that sin is more than a "religious issue." It touches all of man's existence—disjointing and warping his world. It poisons and pollutes and stains where it flows—a people, their society's fabric, or an entire economic order.

Sin results in death. It is an ultimate issue because it ultimately issues in ruin—the ruination of everyone and everything.

Something must be done about sin. It cannot be swept under a carpet. It has to be dealt with. God says so: "For the wages of sin is death" (Romans 6:23). All the rest of the world around us is under Satan's power and control, doomed forever for sins.

Something must be done about sin. It cannot be swept under a carpet. It has to be dealt with.

Lost without God, without hope, you will perish unless you leave your ways. Why will you die? All of these are contemporary phrases of passages from Romans, from John, from Ephesians, from Luke, from the Old Testament prophet, Ezekiel.

In declaring the penalty of sin, God isn't looking for an opportunity to punish people. He doesn't get tough on sin because He wants to get even. To the contrary, He is warning us of a fatal condition: Man's system is poisoned by sin. His survival, happiness, and fulfillment require an antidote.

But there could only be one antidote: blood sacrifice. The Law's exacting demands for sacrifices taught graphic lessons about sin's seriousness—lessons that had to be learned—for man's soul, indeed society's potential survival, was at stake.

SIN IS EXPENSIVE. THAT IS THE SECOND LESSON THE Law taught—how payment for sin could be made. In the animal that was brought as a substitutional sacrifice, the Lord provided another picture.

At the time of creation when God placed a perfect man in a perfect world, He made a contract. "If you sin, death will be the result" (Genesis 3:3, paraphrased). That contract still stands. That is why sin cannot be ignored or excused. Its price is death. But herein lies a problem. If a man pays the price of his sin himself (that is, he dies for his sin) then obviously, he will not be present to enjoy the benefits of the price having been paid. So into the dilemma of man's inability to pay his sin's unavoidable debt, the genius of God's plan was introduced. He provided a substitute.

In the lesson book of the original covenant, the substitutes He provided were animals. This temporary plan has created ideological difficulties for those to whom the sacrificial system seems inhumane. But upon closer study, only ignorance or small-mindedness can indict God for insensitivity toward His own creation. The charges that the Old Testament sacrifices were "just so much blood letting, just another ancient cult," do not stand the test of honest investigation.

There is a vast difference between the sacrificial system God gave Moses and the sacrifices of paganism in the ancient world. Given time, pagan ritual inevitably resorted to human sacrifice—children thrown into flames, virgins cast into volcanoes, youths drowned alive to appease demon gods. Paganism's blood sacrifices involved cruelty, superstition, flagellation, and violence.

In contrast, God's lesson plan used animals, insisted on their being killed without cruelty, and dignified humans by divorcing them from superstition. The teaching was a positive stepping-stone toward man's understanding of sacrifice. Consider God's sacrificial system:

1. The sacrifice was always made mercifully. The creature's death was instantaneous and virtually painless.

2. The sacrifice was not wasted. For the most part, the meat was used as food for both the worshiper and the priest. This is a fact too few realized. There was a joyful feast, celebrating the forgiveness.

3. The sacrifices were readily available within the resources of all the people. Even the poorest could afford the wholly acceptable smaller offerings.

There is no way a thoughtful person can criticize the method God used to teach about substitutionary sacrifice. It was specific and demanding, but it was neither brutal nor loveless. And it did teach how the payment for sin would be made.

Still, though the most exacting obedience was rendered, the lesson-learning did not solve the ultimate problem. Hebrews 9:9 tells us that even in the midst of observing the Law's traditions, there was never a perfection with "regard to the conscience."

The regular performance of the sacrifices became a constant reminder that sin still had not been dealt with conclusively. People knew the sacrifice must be repeated next week, next month, next year. And the repetition of the sacrifice was a constant reminder of sin, an inescapable and unforgettable reality until the Bible says, "the time of reformation" in Christ (Hebrews 9:10).

Diorthosis IS THE NEW TESTAMENT WORD FOR "reformation." Its central meaning relates to the reordering of something that has been shifted from its original position, or a straightening of something that has been bent, or a mending of something that has been shattered. The cultural use of the word in Bible times further enriches our appreciation of the text, for the same word was used in the medical profession to describe the resetting of a broken or shattered bone. In political circles, it was used to describe the setting up of a new kingdom. And in economics, it described the final payment of a debt.

Reformation would make possible the restructuring of all of man's life, the straightening of everything warped, the restoration of life's shattered pieces . . .

Dramatically, in this one word, Scripture outlines what the ultimate, eternal sacrifice would provide when "the time of reformation" would come. Simply summarized, that reformation would make possible the restructuring of all of man's life, the straightening of everything warped, the restoration of life's shattered pieces, and the kingdom of God would bring in a new order of government and make one final payment for man's indebtedness. Hallelujah.

And so the traditions led toward the reformation order, and through their observance mankind was given insight into the forthcoming confrontation with sin that would be faced on man's behalf and fulfilled for man's benefit—by the Visitor.

THE TRANSACTION

9

$\mathcal{M}$artin Burnham and his wife Gracia were mission-aries in the Philippines with New Tribes Missions. As chief pilot for the mission, Martin often would be gone, leaving his wife at the base where she would follow his progress by radio. It was a demanding job but one they loved. They were playing a significant role in helping indigenous people receive God's Word in their own language and come to know His Son, Jesus, as their Savior. The rigors of missionary life were exhausting. So when the opportunity came to celebrate their eighteenth wedding anniversary at a plush Philippine resort, they both jumped at the chance.

What had been a romantic getaway unexpectedly turned terrifying. At 4:30 in the morning, Martin awoke to

loud pounding on the door of their room. He stumbled
from bed to see who was there. Before he could open the
door, three men carrying M-16 rifles barged in and took
him. All too soon he would learn their identity as Abu
Sayyaf terrorists—a radical group affiliated with Osama
bin Laden and committed to the establishment of an inde-
pendent Muslim state in the southern islands.

Shortly they returned for Gracia, taking her to a boat
where Martin and eighteen others were being held. Without
knowledge of what awaited them or where they were being
led, the hostages were taken out to sea. Several days later,
they arrived at Basilan Island, a well-known training ground
for these notorious rebels. Those familiar with the Abu
Sayyaf had cause to fear for the Burnhams' safety. This was a
group known for beheading their hostages if ransom
demands were not met.

Thus began endless months of a life on the run in the
Philippine jungle. Published reports indicated their captivity
included near-starvation, frequent gun battles, witnessing
cold-hearted murder, and intense soul-searching. God, at
times, seemed to be deaf to their prayers for rescue. The
Burnham's longed to be reunited with their three children.

Although the Philippine army was continually hunting
down the terrorists, the Abu Sayyaf took advantage of the
dense jungle and successfully dodged them. There were
seventeen major skirmishes between the military and the
rebels. But the last one brought unspeakable loss.

The soldiers began shooting just as the Burnhams had stretched out in their hammocks for a nap. Hearing the gunfire, Martin and Gracia dropped to the ground, but not before both were struck. The impact caused Gracia to roll down a muddy incline, coming to rest next to her husband's lifeless body. Fearing for her own safety, she pretended to be dead. When she could no longer hear her captors among the voices, she assumed the military had driven them out. She began to move her arms arousing the attention of the soldiers.

After being held hostage for over a year, Gracia Burnham was finally free. It was a day for which Christians around the world had prayed. But the joy of her release was countered by the agony of what she replayed over and over again in her mind. It was a gruesome scene—Martin's body lying in a pool of blood. She was no longer a captive, but her freedom was not without cost.

It is important to understand that Gracia Burnham's freedom was not the result of dealing with her captor's demands, for ransom money was never paid. But her rescue did require a type of payment. The payment was initiated with a gunfight by which the military engaged the rebels who held her and her husband hostage. In other words, a transaction began. Necessary action was required to get what the military (and the Western world) desired. Sadly, the transaction concluded with an expenditure of blood and the loss of Martin's life.

In the case of our freedom from sin, Christ knew He would have to shed His blood and give His life. It was the only way the ransom could be paid and the full transaction of our rescue accomplished.

HEBREWS 10:12 SAYS, "But this Man, after He had offered one sacrifice for sins forever, sat down at the right hand of God."

Read these three words again: "But this Man." In these three words, our text answers the questions that arose when the reformation was promised. By whom would it come? How would it take place? We are told that Christ would transact the redemption of mankind, not with the blood of animals but with His own blood, once and for all.

Here is a complete transaction, not repeated every year as in the school lessons, but once and for all. And by that culminating action, a provision is announced. He has obtained eternal redemption for us.

In light of our study, these are universe-shaking words.

1. Jesus obtained the eternal redemption of mankind by paying a price through a single and conclusive transaction.

2. That transaction was accomplished with blood—
   His own blood—by which means all transgressions
   under the Law have been covered.

In the parlance of the ancient world, *redemption* was a
word used in the slave market business. The Greek lexicon
defines *redemption* as "buying back a slave or captive
through the paying of a ransom." Our English dictionary
elaborates by defining ransom as "the bringing back of or
release of a captive or seized property by the payment of
money or compliance with other demands." Drama and
dynamics unfold in these words: redemption and ransom,
for they reveal what the Visitor did for us in the shedding of
His blood. For He is "this Man" mentioned—Christ
Jesus—who gave Himself as a ransom for us all.

Simply put, Jesus was the ransom paid for man's
redemption. His blood was the price paid to recover
mankind—the property seized from God's hand. Jesus
came into the marketplace of mankind, found slaves on
the block and freed them at the expense of Himself. And
He is still coming today to people who are enslaved,
hooked in a thousand different ways; hooked by pride to a
never-ending treadmill in pursuit of social acceptance,
success, and material possessions; hooked by lust into
pursuing the latest trends or easiest relationship, hoping to
satisfy the sensuous cravings of debased tastes; hooked by

intimidating fears, haunting lies from the past, crushing depression, unceasing pain, or unquenchable hate.

Dear one, this is the marketplace to which Jesus comes and it is there that He offers His blood as the ransom payment. And as our Mediator, the One making the transaction, He brings us promise and hope. You can, I can, mankind can, we all can be unhooked and set free by the payment of Christ's blood. The payment has already been made and right now makes possible the new order.

Diorthosis.

A full recovery.

A new kingdom.

A full recovery and complete liberty.

Diorthosis. A full recovery. A new kingdom. A full recovery and complete liberty.

THE MEANING OF THE BLOOD OF JESUS IS EXPANDED even further when we consider the physical qualities of human blood, for then we find that redemptive applications abound.

First, the word *blood* is a definitive term used in referring to a person's ethnic or social background. For example, when someone asks, "Where'd your family come from?" or "What's your nationality?" a common answer is

"Oh, we're of . . ." and then they will answer with German, English, African, Oriental blood, or whatever. So blood denotes descent, and due to human prejudices sometimes becomes that which can divide people. The prejudice may be racial or it may be nothing more than family favoritism. After all, the old saw grinds, "blood runs thicker than water."

Mankind was never intended for such small-hearted, small-minded separatism. When Paul addressed the Athenian philosophers, he said this of God, the Creator of mankind: "And He has made from one blood every nation of men" (Acts 17:26). And it is a fact. Though the world is filled with myriad nationalities, languages, cultures, and physical features, the essential sameness and interchangeability of human blood is constant. Although the Bible affirmed this fact long ago, human superstition and prejudice have been ignorant of and resistant to it until relatively recent scientific research validated it.

To this day that physical fact pictures a spiritual reality, for the blood of Christ is the ultimate unifier. His blood transforms the human heart and produces unity, not only with God, but the possibility of a social integration that makes all believers "one body"—neither slave nor free man, as the Bible says, neither Jew nor Gentile, neither male nor female. This is the way Jesus' blood brings people of various races and cultures together, through the love of the Father and the workings of the Holy Spirit.

In offering His blood as a covering for people of every nation, Jesus has identified Himself with all mankind, but He paid the price of every man's salvation with blood that is common to every man, regardless of ethnic descent. Therefore, it becomes unsurprising and appropriate that eternal worship will be offered to Jesus by the redeemed from every nation, every kingdom, every tribe, and every tongue. Their unified theme will be the one sacrifice He has made for them and the price paid for their release in a blood common to them all. Worthy is the Lamb who has washed us with His blood.

> *Worthy is the Lamb who has washed us with His blood.*

BLOOD NOT ONLY IDENTIFIES, BUT BLOOD VERIFIES. It is often used or employed as an instrument of verification. Though someone may say in jest, "What do you want, a signature in blood?" the fact remains that documents have been signed that way. To this day in some cultures, a covenant may be sealed by the cutting of flesh and the intermingling of blood by tribal representatives. It acknowledges a covenant and verifies a point of union.

And though vastly different from primitive ritual, Jesus signed the deed of man's salvation. An old song sings:

He signed the deed with His atoning blood.

He ever lives to make His promise good.

Should all the hosts of hell march in,

To make a second claim,

They all march out at the mention of His name.

BLOOD ALSO CONSUMMATES. IN HIS MASTERPIECE OF tribute at Gettysburg, Abraham Lincoln employed phrases that are still unforgettable. He referred to those whose blood was shed as having given "the last full measure of devotion," and he asserted what all recognize: Nothing more consummately declares a full commitment than a person willing to die for a cause.

Jesus demonstrates that. In shedding His blood voluntarily, He testifies to God's absolute commitment to us. In dying, Jesus affirms His full devotion to us. He wasn't forced to die, but He chose to do it.

Therein lies not only the willingness for the full gift that will pay for us, but an enormous statement about the worth placed upon us. And now that the transaction is fully accomplished, the price fully paid, you and I can stand before God with assurance, for our sin has not been swept aside. It has been disannulled.

By the power of Christ's conclusive sacrifice, once and for all, my conscience may stand washed free of sin, guilt, and shame—not that it was forgotten but that it has been dissipated completely through the power of the cross. His full measure of devotion has completely settled a new contract. It is established and in force. He is alive, and I'm forgiven. And so are you. Amen!

THE TRANSFUSION

10

*W*illiam Cowper (pronounced Cooper) was six years old when his mother died. Without her to care for his domestic needs, William's father sent his grieving son to a boarding school. While at school, the slight-of-build boy was the object of badgering and bullying. His sensitive nature internalized the pain of the physical and emotional abuse. As he grew older, William had thoughts of becoming a lawyer. But the rigors of law school along with the unaddressed issues of his past ambushed him. William had two unhappy love affairs, and struggled throughout his life with a sense of inferiority. Twice he tried to commit suicide, unsuccessful in his attempts. By the time William turned twenty-five, he had been committed to a mental hospital.

Conscious of his failures in life and aware that he had transgressed the laws of God both knowingly and unknowingly, William was often heard crying out, "My sin! My sin! Oh, for some fountain open for my cleansing!" It was during his hospitalization that William discovered that such a fountain actually existed.

While under the care of a Christian physician named Dr. Cotton, William learned of the saving grace of Jesus. As he learned of the Savior's sacrifice on the cross and the redemptive nature of Jesus' blood, he understood that the fountain that symbolized the Cross was the only fountain capable of washing guilt and sin away.

Taking pen in hand, William described his experience:

The happy period which was to shake off my fetters and afford me a clear opening of the free mercy of God in Christ Jesus was now arrived. I flung myself into a chair near the window, and, seeing a Bible there, ventured once more to apply to it for comfort and instruction. The first verses I saw were in the third chapter of Romans: 'Being justified freely by his grace through the redemption that is in Christ Jesus, whom God hath set forth to be a propitiation, through faith in his blood, to manifest his righteousness.' Immediately I received strength to believe, and the full beams of the Sun of Righteousness shone on me.

I saw the sufficiency of the atonement He had made, my pardon in His blood, and the fullness and completeness of His justification. In a moment, I believed and received the gospel.

WILLIAM FORSOOK HIS EARLIER DREAMS OF PRACTICING law and became a well-respected poet in England. At the age of forty while contemplating the supernatural and timeless power of the Savior's blood, he wrote a hymn that chronicled his conversion.

It wasn't the only Christian hymn he wrote. In fact, before William died at the age of sixty-nine he had established himself as one of the more prolific hymn writers of the eighteenth century. But it is likely the lyrics that flow out of his conversion that most people associate with him. In the words of "There Is a Fountain," he has provided a vocabulary of faith for those who have experienced a similar spiritual cleansing.

There is a fountain filled with blood drawn from
        Emmanuel's veins;
And sinners plunged beneath that flood lose all their
        guilty stains.
Lose all their guilty stains, lose all their guilty stains;
And sinners plunged beneath that flood lose all their
        guilty stains.
The dying thief rejoiced to see that fountain in his day;

And there have I, though vile as he, washed all my sins away.

Washed all my sins away, washed all my sins away;

And there have I, though vile as he, washed all my sins away.

Dear dying Lamb, Thy precious blood shall never lose its
    power

Till all the ransomed church of God be saved,
    to sin no more.

Be saved, to sin no more, be saved, to sin no more;

Till all the ransomed church of God be saved, to sin no more.

E'er since, by faith, I saw the stream
    Thy flowing wounds supply,

Redeeming love has been my theme, and shall be till I die.

    And shall be till I die, and shall be till I die;

Redeeming love has been my theme, and shall be till I die.

William Cowper, though plagued with emotional and mental illnesses, had no difficulty accepting the terms of how the dying Lamb's blood provides a once-for-all transfusion to those who are dying without salvation. The blood of Christ alone was capable of cleansing him from sin and infusing him with power.

Yes, transfusion is the ideal metaphor for how Christ's blood impacts those who acknowledge His sacrifice on the cross. But for the sake of review, allow me to remind you what I meant by it.

Transfusion. The transfer of blood from one person to another.

Transfusion. The sustaining of the afflicted, sick, or injured.

Through Christ's blood humankind is afforded a supply of life that frees us to break dependency on lesser things.

Without the power of Christ's blood within, man may resort to other power sources for his system—a spoonful of heroin, a bottle of vodka, a stop at a massage parlor, some other social joyride, or perhaps a quest for more sophisticated and socially acceptable forms of input. Whether respectable or not in one way or another, everyone seems to be crying for "a fix," for the multitude, in fact, does need

Whether respectable or not in one way or another, everyone seems to be crying for "a fix."

exactly that: to be fixed; to be put together again.

A more satisfying, durable answer for this need is in a new dimension of living, one with resources and treasure from an inheritance yet untapped—an eternal inheritance. The moment one receives Christ's new life, eternal life begins—a life eternal not only in its quantity of promise but also in its quality. And the bequest of an eternal inheritance begins to affect our present circumstance. Now, this blood-bought inheritance involves actual resources. Just as a relative leaves funds, property, or articles of value to help a person improve his present situation, so the blood of

Christ provides an instant availability of resources to fill life with value and worth. It is that input, that transfusion, which makes deceiving and destructive substitutes not only undesirable but unnecessary.

Jesus is saying, "Come to Me. My blood has purchased an inheritance that offers both provision and release—My life to fulfill and free your life."

WHAT DOES BLOOD DO? IN THE PHYSICAL REALM human blood accomplishes three functions:

1. Blood purifies. It gathers impurities from various parts of the body and transports them to organs where the purification process takes place.

2. Blood nourishes. Food that has been ingested is assimilated into the blood, which carries nourishment to other parts of the body.

3. Blood helps resist infection. It contains the cells that resist organisms hostile to the human body.

All three of these functions—purification, nourishment, resisting infection—can be translated into spiritual dynamics when they flow to us through the transfusion that is offered us through the blood of Christ.

1. There is purification through transfusion. You and I have been born into a race with blood tainted by sin. The Word declares there is a power that flows to us through the blood of Christ. If we will allow a transfusion of His life into ours, it can set in motion a transformation, an ongoing purification of our lives. As 1 John 1:7 puts it, "The blood of Jesus Christ His Son cleanses us from all sin."

2. There is nourishment through transfusion. Jesus said, "Unless you eat the flesh of the Son of Man and drink His blood, you have no life in you" (John 6:53). Jesus interpreted these words by describing them as the teaching of a spiritual truth, not a physical one. The nourishment is real, but it is our invisible inner being which is being fed through Christ's body and blood. He calls us to the table of Communion where the composite spiritual truth He taught speaks to us. "This is His body, broken for you and His blood, shed for you. Eat and drink" (Mark 14:22–25). And a transfusion of His life and power will fill you to nourish you with strength to meet the challenges of every day.

3. We can gain resistance through transfusion. Revelation 12:11 refers to times like ours when satanic forces attack on every hand. Into that spiritual conflict, the Holy Spirit of truth sends a promise: "And they overcame him [the adversary, the devil] by the blood of the Lamb." Here is power to resist the conspiracies of hell, the works of the Devil. The legions of darkness are confounded by the blood of Christ. It bewildered them at Calvary and it will break their stratagems today.

THERE IS NO BETTER WAY TO USE THE POWER OF Christ's blood to resist the devil than to sing about it. In concluding this portion of our study of the might and miracles in the blood of Christ, I invite you to do so. Think through what poets and hymn writers have been declaring across the years. The history of the redeemed in Christ is filled with evidence. God has always had a people who understood the power of the blood of Christ. They have written about it magnificently for centuries. We've already met William Cowper, but he is only one of many whose lyrics paint the imagery of the Visitor's blood.

In 1775, Augustus Toplady wrote, "Rock of Ages, cleft for me, let me hide myself in thee." The cleft rock is analogous

to the slain Lamb, cut open in sacrifice for us. The writer
continues: "Let the water and the blood from thy wounded
side which flowed be of sin a double cure. Save from wrath
and make me pure."

The dual dynamic of the redemptive transaction is
declared:

> I am saved from the wrath of judgment.
> I am purified by Christ's life flowing into my life.

In the 1800's, Robert Lowry put it in these words,
beginning with a declaration of our absolution from the
penalty of past sin:

> What can wash away my sin?
> Nothing but the blood of Jesus.
> What can make me whole again?
> Nothing but the blood of Jesus.

Then Lowry pens the truth of the transforming power
of the blood in its present process of bringing us into
wholeness:

> O, precious is the flow,
> That makes me white as snow.
> No other fount I know,

Nothing but the blood of Jesus.

This is Edward Mote's nineteenth century testament:

My hope is built on nothing less,
Than Jesus' blood and righteousness.
I dare not trust the sweetest frame,
But wholly lean on Jesus' name.

The chorus of that great hymn ignites with exploding absolute confidence:

On Christ the solid rock I stand,
All other ground is sinking sand.

Another verse from this hymn resounds the certainty of our strength through the blood of Christ:

His oath, His covenant, His blood,
Support me in the whelming flood.
When all around my soul gives way,
He then is all my hope and stay.

It was Lewis Jones whose lyrics help us sing of the blood's power to provide an ongoing point of present participation in Jesus' victory. He wrote:

Would you be free from your burden of sin?
There's power in the blood, power in the blood.
Would you o'er evil a victory win?
There's wonderful power in the blood.

And how many of us have sung:

There is power, power, wonder-working power,
In the precious blood of the Lamb.

More contemporarily, Andraé Crouch has given us these words concerning the blood of Christ:

For it reaches to the highest mountain,
It flows to the lowest valley,
The blood that gives me strength from day to day,
It will never lose its power.

And so I was moved in my own private time of worship recently to write these words:

Cleansing power,
Purge this hour,
Wash my heart and all sin erase.
Blood of Jesus, flow and free us,
Lead us, Lord, to Your resting place.

In the blood of Jesus, loved one, we have come to the heart of eternal salvation. Its power transcends that one moment of agony two thousand years ago. The blood draining from that ultimate Man's body is more than symbolic of Jesus' supreme act of love in dying for us. It is the Son of God, the Savior, releasing a life-begetting force to us today. It is forgiving today, and it is triumphant today. It is purifying today. It is nurturing today. It is resistant to the powers of hell today.

Christ's blood penetrates all history. No longer does anyone need to live beneath sin's guilt and condemnation. And no longer do we need to fear the repeated reminders flashed by either our memory or our enemy. An inheritance of love and power has been bequeathed—an inheritance to us. A transaction of consummate triumph has been concluded. And because of the blood, we have embraced the prospect of life new in Him and forever with Him.

Praise the name of Jesus.

HIS DEATH—
THE CRUX OF THE CROSS

11

*M*ost every American can sing the words to "The Star-Spangled Banner" from memory. But not many know the dramatic story behind the song. It was written by a thirty-five-year-old Washington lawyer by the name of Francis Scott Key during a time of horrendous conflict and amazing courage.

When the British had invaded the nation's capital in August of 1814, they had set fire to the Capitol building and the White House. They also had kidnapped a much-loved elderly physician by the name of William Beanes. When Key learned that his friend was being detained on a British flagship in Chesapeake Bay, he headed to Baltimore. Since there was the likelihood that Dr. Beanes could be hanged,

Key used his legal experience in an attempt to secure his friend's release. With the help of Col. John Skinner, an American agent for prisoner exchange, both men set out on a small boat to meet the Royal Navy.

On board the British flagship, the officers were very kind to Key and Skinner. They agreed to release Dr. Beanes. However, the three men were not permitted to return to Baltimore. The British had begun an all-out assault on Fort McHenry. The three Americans were placed aboard an American ship and instructed to wait behind the British fleet. From a distance of several miles, Key and his friends watched the Royal Navy bombard the American fort for twenty-five continuous hours before pulling back.

Although the explosions could be heard from where Key stood, the extent of devastation and casualties was not visible through the smoke and haze. Nonetheless, with the help of a telescope he was able to make out the American flag that continued to wave above the fort in the dawn's early light. To his amazement, the soldiers at Fort McHenry had been victorious. They had not surrendered.

Visitors to the Smithsonian Museum of American History can see the flag that flew over Fort McHenry when Francis Scott Key wrote "The Star-Spangled Banner" in 1814. The original flag measured forty-two feet by thirty feet. No wonder Francis Scott Key was able to see the flag from his position several miles out to sea.

But how could a flag that size be supported on Fort McHenry's wooden flagpole, 189 feet in the air? National Park Rangers discovered the answer in 1958, while excavating nine feet underground near the entrance to the fort. Two oak timbers, eight feet by eight feet, joined as a crossbeam. The enormous cross grounded Old Glory and kept the flag flying.

That American flag is not the only thing supported by a cross. The Gospel, Christ's message to us, is grounded in a cross as well. Without Good Friday, there is no Easter Sunday. Without the cross, there's not much reason to make reference to a manger. The death of Christ is the axis on which the significance of the Visitor's contribution hinges.

While Christ's resurrection is the most triumphant event in history, His death was certainly the most decisive. In His dying, Jesus totally altered the power of death forever.

Death does not merely involve the moment a human being takes his last breath. Death is a process of disruptive intrusion into God's original order set in motion the moment we take our first breath. By reason of man's fall, life has become a relentless process of decay. A fundamental hopelessness resides within most of mankind because of this penalty of man's sin. Death may be rationalized, philosophized, schematized, or ritualized, but inescapably, beyond all humanistic efforts at successfully coping with it, death is realized.

Furthermore, the death that inevitably occurs, besides a man's certain physical demise, is manifested in many other ways in the details of his lifetime. Death comes in the everyday circumstances and events of our living: visions die, health decays, hopes and dreams fade, relationships wither and often die. A lifetime of dying confronts every person.

A lifetime of dying confronts every person.

But Jesus Christ has come to invade every form of death and to infuse it with His life. He is capable of doing that because of His own dying and in that dying, He absorbed all the power of death in Himself.

In His body, death was swallowed up. In submitting to the torment of Calvary, He mastered the tormentor. He bore in Himself the full strike of the blade of death and received into Himself all the bitter fruit due to the sinners of the world. Somehow, in one mighty transference, all of the delinquent accounts of the history of human sin and failure were paid by His sinless person. He received the agony of our penalty and provided the ecstasy of our deliverance.

It is because of His own sinlessness that He was capable of doing this. Only the magnitude of an unencroached upon, untainted soul could absorb the awesome dimension of sin that Christ encountered on the cross. The sins of the entire human race engulfed Him, but death could not hold Him. In God's Son was found a sinlessness that could take on the guilt of all humanity and still survive an encounter with divine justice. By the sheer power of His holy sinlessness, Christ exhausted the power of that sin, broke the power of death, and came through in triumph.

The decisiveness of Jesus' death is reflected in the definition it has given to three terms in our language: crux, crises, and crossroads.

Crux as you may know is the Latin word for "cross." And I wonder if we would use that word in common vernacular if it weren't for the fact that the force and impact of the word has been defined by the Cross of the Lord Jesus. How often we hear someone say, "Get to the crux of the matter," meaning "penetrate to the core, and bypass the inconsequential." But it seems that idiom depends on Christ's cross for definition, for it was there that the central issues of the human race were confronted and settled. Sin was paid for and forgiven; death was faced and banished.

Crisis is derived from the Greek word for "judgment." That is what the cross was—a place of judgment for sin.

Hebrews 9:27 says, "And as it is appointed for men to

die once, but after this the judgment." When He came to that moment of judgment, Jesus kept an appointment for us—our appointment with death as a penalty for sin. That is an appointment we could never have kept and survived. We will all keep an appointment with biological death but we will never have to withstand the judgment that ordinarily accompanies it. Why? Because Christ faced it for us. He bore it all for you and for me. Hallelujah!

So both words, *crux* and *crisis,* seem to derive their primary weight in force from the definition that has been given to them by the Cross of Christ, on which He dealt with man's central problem—sin—and vanquished man's central fear—death.

The word *crossroads* indicates a point of decision; a point where the future is determined. And at Calvary, we come to the ultimate crossroads. It is there we face three of the most staggering realities this world has ever known:

1. God's Son died on the cross.

2. Man's sin was judged in the cross.

3. God's justice was satisfied at the cross.

Thus, what a person does in the face of Calvary's realities is a conclusive determining factor for every aspect of life. It is a crossroads, here and hereafter.

First, God's son died on the cross. Don't make the mistake of supposing Jesus to be simply an historic personality, an influential leader, a moral teacher, a gifted prophet, or a dramatic miracle worker. He is not just a noble martyr who excites admiration through the centuries either, by His willingness to die for His convictions.

Instead, the significance of the cross is that the Son of God died there. The only begotten offspring of the Almighty One of heaven, Jesus is unique. No one like Him has been born before or since. He is specifically, especially, and singly the Savior

The only begotten offspring of the Almighty One of heaven, Jesus is unique.

sent from above, and at the cross He is executing His purpose in coming and fulfilling the primary reason for His visit here. He who came, the Visitor, to share the experience of life with us, submitted to death for us. Since we, God's children, are human beings made of flesh and blood, He became flesh and blood too (Hebrews 2:14). It was an incredible proposition, but He accepted it. And the Cross of Jesus Christ towers above all history by reason of that primary fact.

And secondly, as we said, Man's sin was judged on the cross. We discussed earlier how the sin of mankind cannot be lightly dismissed with a wave of the hand. Forgiveness is not easy, sin has to be dealt with, and the forgiveness that has resulted was not easily secured, but it is freely available because His work on the cross truly and thoroughly dealt with the seriousness of sin.

Sadly, if concerned at all, the world has become convinced that the only thing necessary to dispense with sin is for someone to observe a moment of regret, a sincere "I'm sorry." Or many believe that some cosmic largesse (that is, heavenly generosity) should accept the appeal: "Look, God, so I failed. Don't be too hard on me. After all, I am only human."

To man's way of thinking, such appeals should handle the problem of sin. But sin has to be dealt with more seriously and completely than that, because at the core of the universal structure of things, something has been violated. Life is disjointed and disfigured and deadened. Sin is the reason for all of it, and it must be dealt with thoroughly. This need is not because God is vindictive, but because He has lovingly looked upon His fallen race and concluded, "If sin isn't dealt with, if it is not neutralized, they will never be able to enjoy the fulfillment I have for them and the destiny for which they were created."

And so it is in that light, we can understand the Cross of Jesus Christ, for that was God's means of dealing with sin. By this one Man, through this one act, God judged sin conclusively. Romans 5:15 says, ". . . For if by the one man's offense many died, much more the grace of God and the gift by the grace of the one Man, Jesus Christ, abounded to many." That obedience was Christ's, and the specific moment of obeying was in His submitting to death on the cross.

Then, as we noted thirdly, God's justice was satisfied at the cross. When we speak of God's justice being satisfied in the death of Christ, let's not think of it as a matter of God saying, "I need to be appeased," as though He were a vengeful deity exploding with tantrums until His whims were served. Instead, let's recognize that we are dealing with a God who is the essence of holiness, justice, and righteousness, so much so, that anything contrary to His nature cannot survive the blazing purity of His presence. Yet it is for that presence, that union with Him in intimacy, that He created man. So a dilemma presents itself. The Creator desires the presence and partnership of man, but the creature has fallen from the relationship, the likeness that was given him that would allow for unity in intimacy. The Just One desires the companionship of the one who has unjustly violated trust with Him. He longs for him to return to His side, yet He must insist, "My justice must be satisfied not because I wish vengeance, but because I cannot change My nature. I cannot be less than just any more that I can be less than loving."

God cannot lie, nor can He use any other means than justice to deal with sin. And the cosmic order is that sin means death to the sinner. "The soul who sins shall die" (Ezekiel 18:20).

But the Son of God is being lifted up on Calvary. And whoever believes in Him shall not perish but shall have eternal life. Here at the cross, God is judging sin in an action that will allow Him to embrace man to His heart again. God so loved the world, He gave His only begotten Son (John 3:16). And the love that requires justice miraculously exhausts its wrath on a volunteering substitute—the One being in the universe able to survive that judgment—Himself, His Son.

AND SO IT IS THAT THE CROSS DESTROYED THE POWER of death. But the Cross not only means the victory of forgiveness for sin through God's justice having been satisfied, it also provides deliverance from the power of sin as it seeks to destroy life. "That through death," Hebrews 2:14 says, "He might destroy him who had the power of death." The Cross represents a total breakthrough in the entire order of things that bind mankind.

In *The Chronicles of Narnia,* C. S. Lewis has given us a series of beautiful and simple concepts that develop in such a story form that spiritual realities become vibrantly alive. In no way are those stories tedious or preachy, but they run on as a stirring adventure, enticing and entertaining readers of all ages. The opening book, *The Lion, the*

Witch, and the Wardrobe, is an introduction to the mystical, magical land of Narnia, where animals talk with people, horses fly, and a witch, who is the epitome of evil, lives in conflict with a lion named Aslan.

Readers shortly discern that Aslan is clearly meant to symbolize Jesus Christ, the Lion of Judah. And Lewis as much as names him Jesus before one finishes the seven *Narnia* volumes. One exchange in the first book states as clearly as anyone could describe the destruction of death's power when Jesus died upon the cross. The story relates it this way:

Narnia (the land) is held in the witch's evil spell of constant winter. Four children have come to the land and they seek to break the spell. Edmund, one of the four, has turned traitor against the others and selfishly aligned himself with the witch. The children had earlier warned Edmund against his obvious inclination to side with the witch, but Edmund, like you and me, continues to go against what he knows he ought to be and do and finally sells out to her evil and betrays the other children. Then Edmund's bitter moment of truth arrives. The witch, triumphant in her evil mastery over the boy, confronts Aslan the Lion with Edmund's guilt. The other children are looking on.

"Aslan, you have a traitor here."

"But his offense was not against you."

"But Aslan, have you forgotten the deep magic?" the witch asks.

Aslan answers gravely, "Let us say I have forgotten. Tell us of the deep magic."

"Tell you," says the witch, her voice growing suddenly shriller, "tell you what is written in letters as deep as the spear is long in the trunk of the world ash tree? Tell you what is written on the very table of stone which stands beside us? Tell you what is engraved on the scepter of the emperor beyond the sea? You at least, Aslan, know that magic which the emperor put into Narnia at the very beginning. You know that every traitor belongs to me as lawful prey and that for every treachery, I have the right to kill."

The witch's statement is a pointed summary of what is true on our planet, and what was written into the very structure of things from the beginning. Genesis 2:17 says, "For in the day that you eat of it you shall surely die."

Death does not come to mankind by mere biological processes, nor does it come at the hands of an angry God. It is the direct result of man's outright disobedience in an act of sin, action which has plunged him into a warped realm that is administrated and directed by "him who had the power of death, that is, the devil" (Hebrews 2:14).

As seen in Lewis's witch, nothing delights our adversary more than to exact what is his legal right. To administer death to all who have turned against "the emperor," that is, the most high God, the "Living One."

To continue the story, Aslan offers himself to the witch in the place of Edmund. And as he does, the witch and her lackeys seize Aslan. They gleefully bind him with ropes. They tear off his mane and they brutally slay him.

Susan and Lucy, Edmund's two sisters, watch this scene in horror, from a place in hiding, unable to believe what has happened. Later, after the witch and her followers are gone, the girls see a legion of small mice swarming over Aslan's lifeless body, chewing at the ropes that bind him to the table where he has been slain. Grief-stricken and overwhelmed with hopelessness the girls fall asleep. They are awakened by a loud noise and, looking to the stone on which Aslan was killed, they discover his dead carcass is gone. The ropes that bound him are scattered. The stone on which he was killed is broken. Lucy and Susan are filled with bewilderment until suddenly Aslan appears. As he approaches them, a radiance shines about him. The great lion's mane is back and with every step he takes, flowers rise to bloom in his tracks. The winter spell that held Narnia in its clutches is beginning to thaw, and in the midst of their joyful reunion one of the girls asks, "Aslan, what does it all mean?"

This is his reply, and it is the point of the story's retelling: Aslan speaks,

> "It means that though the witch knew the deep magic, there is a magic deeper still which she did not know. Her knowledge only goes back until the dawn of time, but if she could have looked a little further back into the stillness and darkness before the dawn of time she would have read there a different incantation. She would have known that when a willing victim who had committed no treachery was killed in a traitor's stead the table would crack, and death itself would start working backwards."

OH, LOVED ONES, I KNOW NO CLEARER illustration—the significance of the death of Christ. Christianity's finest theologians are surpassed by these words from a children's story. For, simply spoken, Jesus became that willing victim: "For He made Him who knew no sin to be sin for us, that we might become the righteousness of God in Him" (2 Corinthians 5:21). And as Hebrews 2:14 trumpets the truth: By His death, Jesus destroyed him who had the power of death, and set the power of death in reverse. The deadening, paralyzing grip of all that clutches and controls us was broken. The yoke which locked life to death laws has been cast aside, man's winter of discontent has begun to thaw, and the spring-time of His deliverance has come because the Visitor has become our Redeemer.

Praise His holy name.

ALL'S OUT, IN FREE

12

$\mathcal{T}$odd Beamer and his wife Lisa returned home to New Jersey from a weeklong getaway in Rome on Monday afternoon, September 10, 2001. The thirty-two-year-old executive with Oracle Corporation hated to leave the very next morning for a business meeting in California. He'd been gone from his two young boys and wanted to spend time with them. Besides, leaving Lisa alone with all there was to take care of after a week's absence didn't seem very caring of his five-months-pregnant-wife. But Todd knew it was a necessary trip, and he'd be back that same night.

Leaving before dawn on Tuesday, Todd drove to the Newark airport where he left his car and waited to board United Flight #93 for San Francisco. Settling into his seat,

Todd made a couple of calls on his cell phone and then pulled out his Tom Clancy novel. A bookmark engraved with the Lord's Prayer marked the page where he had left off.

Although Flight #93 was delayed for forty minutes, once it left the gate a smooth take-off into cloudless blue skies soon gave the passengers reason to expect a smooth and uneventful westbound journey. About the time the plane entered Cleveland airspace, Todd realized the pilot had turned the plane sharply to the south and slightly east. They were no longer heading toward California. Within minutes chaos unfolded before his eyes. As a man with a foreign accent identified himself as the pilot, two members of the crew were pulled from the flight deck appearing to be dead. The passengers were herded to the back of the plane. Flight #93 had been hijacked!

While Todd tried to make sense out of what was taking place, frightened passengers were using their cell phones to call loved ones. That's when they learned about the attacks on the Twin Towers of the World Trade Center and the Pentagon. Piecing together a likely scenario, it was all too obvious that the men who had commandeered the plane were guiding the flight toward another target near the nation's capital. Although the passengers didn't know the exact location the terrorists were planning to crash into, they were aware of one thing—they were likely about to die. Their uneventful flight to San Francisco was anything but.

Todd didn't want to risk upsetting his pregnant wife by calling her with details of the possible disaster. Rather, he used the AirFone in the back of a seat pocket and called a GTE operator. When he described the situation aboard Flight #93, the operator transferred the call to her supervisor. For the following twenty minutes, Todd relayed a blow-by-blow account of what he was observing. Aware that he was going to die, he asked the woman on the other end of the line to relay a message of love and farewell to his wife. He then asked the supervisor if she would pray the Lord's Prayer with him. She consented.

For Todd, the Lord's Prayer was anything but a religious rabbit's foot. His personal faith in Jesus Christ was central to his life. His parents had taught him that familiar prayer (and its meaning) from the time he was a preschooler. The fact that he chose to keep the prayer on a bookmark was indicative of Todd's trust in the Heavenly Father.

After praying the most-loved prayer with a perfect stranger, Todd gave indication that some sort of an ambush was being planned by some of the passengers. From what the GTE supervisor could tell, it appeared Todd was helping to plot this counterattack. She heard him say, "Are you ready? Let's roll!" It wasn't long thereafter that the phone went dead. It was later learned that the plane had nose-dived into a rural field in Somerset County, Pennsylvania. The unknown target, a hundred or so miles further east, was never reached.

Todd's memorable phrase, "Let's Roll!" has become a verbal touchstone to the courage exhibited on Flight #93. It was a rallying point for those passengers mustering their courage and confidence in the face of their greatest fears. But Todd wasn't facing his greatest fear. He was sound in the knowledge that His Lord and Savior had already triumphed over death and robbed the grave of its power. Live or die on that September morning, Todd Beamer knew he had no reason to fear. His victory had already been won.

THERE'S ANOTHER PHRASE THAT COMES TO MIND. It's one I used when I was a youngster playing hide-and-seek: "Ally, ally, out's in free!" I remember the words so well. What was really being said was that everybody who was out, is now in free. "All's out, in free."

The call of Christ to come into His light takes me back to that hide-and-seek game-ender that we called out as children, "All's out, in free."

Of course, His is more than a child's game of hide-and-seek. But the fear of being found by God in our sin, or being bound by Satan with our sin, can be stopped. His words are life—all's out, in free. "If the Son makes you free, you shall be free indeed" (John 8:36). But the fear of death has closed the door to the light of those words for many. Hebrews 2:15 says, "Those who through fear of death were all their lifetime subject to bondage." But Jesus' death has come to deliver us from the fear of death, from the fear and necessity of bondage.

We need to define these words "fear of death," for they address far more than a human shudder at the prospect of dying, more than the fantasy of a screaming descent in a doomed jetliner. The fear of death is not the struggle with a phantom threatening your physical demise. Rather, this phrase describes the devastating sense of hopelessness that often torments people:

There is nothing that gnaws at a person's soul more cruelly than the grinding spirit of futility.

the haunting sense that nothing is going to change; that no turnaround will come; that the worst will happen; that no one will care afterward. There is nothing that gnaws at a person's soul more cruelly than the grinding spirit of futility; the fear of death.

People come to dead-end streets, and it is there that they meet death-fear—suffering on a bed of pain, struggling with an ailing marriage, trying to survive a business setback, wondering if the ache of divorce will ever leave.

That same fear sneers when someone doubts whether the tide will turn, if the sun will break through, that the depression will leave, that the habit will be conquered, or if the hurt will ever go away.

When one begins to believe that nothing will ever change, the fear of death has beaten him—temporarily—until the message of the deliverance available through Jesus' death gains his trust.

And we discover the climaxing conquest. You see, we have discussed the depths of Christ's love and His condescension, the wholeness we can gain through His suffering, the healing that is available through His wounds, and the forgiveness He provides through His blood.

But dear friend, the crowning moment of the hour which He came to fulfill is the one of death. And in that action, for it is an action and not merely an occurrence, Jesus drains death of all its power to contain mankind. He is not only in His death paying the penalty of human sin and breaking the bondage imposed by the serpent's grip, but He is exploding death's power to intimidate, to dictate terms, or to exact tribute upon us at any point in our lives. Because Jesus' body slumped without breath or heartbeat on a cross, death has no more power now. He has risen from the tomb, and He continues to shout to our generation, "I am alive

forevermore and have the keys of hell and of death!"
(Revelation 1:18).

The very fact of His life is the verification that death is a
vanquished foe, and in giving His life to us, He provides a
force in our lives to dominate death in all its manifestations.

How many live in a casket of circumstances?

How many tread through life in a grave-like rut?

How many are tangled in the grave clothes of past experiences or habit?

Dear one, to you, Jesus comes and says, "Don't be
afraid. The end of that which has come upon you is near at
hand. What you feared would never change is shortly to be
overthrown forever."

I VISITED WITH A FRIEND, AN EXCELLENT PASTOR,
whom I have known since our college days together. A
season of frustration had beset him. In response, he had
weakened before temptation. His disappointment with
himself was exceeded only by his embarrassment at his
failure. He left his ministry. He moved his family to another
city. He sought solace in the mountains. He bent his back to
hard labor in an attempt to forget. He doubted the possibility of ever again realizing what he knew to be his life's
God-ordained purpose. Just when it seemed recovery had

begun, a new dimension of depression was engulfing him. At this point, he asked if we could get together to talk. As we conversed, a picture came to my mind—a photograph I sensed to be a God-given scene depicting the condition of his own mind. I saw a pitch-black tunnel, stretching for miles beneath an enormous Everest of a mountain. From the vantage point of my vision I could see my friend, groping at the front wall of the tunnel, digging his way forward. Tears filled his eyes, evidence of a heart despairing with the belief that the mountain was eternal and the tunnel endless. But the scene I was shown was laden with hope, for from the perspective I was being given only a few feet of the tunnel remained. It was about to end in the breakthrough of blessed daylight and a conclusion of the wearying journey through the darkness.

The scene dissolved, and I looked at my friend and said, "Jim, let me describe your feeling and your thinking." I related the picture. I identified his sense of futility with the prospect that nothing would ever be any different. Then I shared the conclusion: "Jim, there are just a few more feet to go. Don't despair. The Lord is wanting you to know that He has taken all futility out of your life's prospect. Things will change. Breakthrough is not far away."

And Jim wept. His tears evidenced at that very minute a returning, heartwarming confidence as the Spirit of God breathed truth into his soul. After some time, he regained his composure and finally spoke: "Jack, I don't know how to thank God for those words. The darkness of my soul has been by itself enough to kill hope. But what has been the most destructive to me, robbing my life of any joy, was the thought, 'Nothing will ever change.' But I know it's a lie, and God's truth has set me free to believe and to hope with certainty." It was only a few weeks until the vision was fulfilled and this man's experience of fresh release in life and light began.

But, you see, Jim's real release began before he actually experienced it weeks later. It began when he saw the vision of the Lord's guaranteed victory. Then the fear of death was broken. His response in faith was not the result of human wisdom or counsel. It was the Holy Spirit Himself bearing witness to the greatest

Jesus Christ has broken the power of death to rule you at any point in your life.

truth mankind can ever know: Jesus Christ has broken the power of death to rule you at any point in your life.

Todd Beamer discovered that truth on September 11, 2001. My friend, Jim, also discovered that truth, and his life was changed.

And for you who read these words with me, you are loved as well, my friend. And I write to you as a loved one, having no idea what your specific need may be as you read this book. But whatever it is, I invite you to come to the cross of Christ. It is there that Jesus has reversed the power of death and brought complete deliverance for you. You no longer need to be trapped, intimidated, or driven by the things resulting from past or present bondage.

He loves you with an everlasting love. Read it again: He loves you with an everlasting love (Jeremiah 31:3, paraphrased).

And because that everlasting love reaches out right now to meet you at any point in your life, I issue this gentle invitation. I invite you to bring that point of problem, sting of stress, the agony of bondage that most troubles you, whatever it may be. With your prayerful imagination, take it in hand right now. Whatever that thing is, place it at the foot of the cross and wait there, and let the light of God's everlasting love and almighty triumph shine on it. Speak your heart openly to Him. And if you wish, use the prayer below, inserting your point of heartfelt need as I lead you. As you do so, pour your heart out in a simple childlike way because the Visitor is coming to visit you right now, to visit you again at your point of suffering with the resources of His triumph over every pain, every wound, all suffering, bondage, and death. Speak to Him.

Father, I bring You (insert your heart's cry now).
I bring You (name what it is that is on your mind,
your heart, your burden).

Father, I bring You (say it).
That the bonds, Father, may be broken.
I bring You (speak your need) that the victory You
offer may be realized.
I bring my fears, my loneliness, and my doubts
(name them to Him).
I renounce any bitterness that I may have entertained
in my heart. (Admit to it without fear of reprisal.
Confession will be releasing.)

And now say to Him:

Jesus, You were pierced through that
I might have a breakthrough.
Release me, dear Lord, as I receive Your freedom,
healing, and deliverance right now. Amen.

And then say:

Jesus, thank You for coming to visit us, for suffering
for us, for Your wounds on our behalf, for Your blood
securing our deliverance, for your cross-destroying
death's fearsome power. We thank and praise You
that You have done all this for us. And we bow with
thanks to rise in anticipating the future, bringing our
praise and our worship, as our life is given back to

> *You, freely, as You have given Yours to us. Holy*
> *Savior, we praise You. Amen and Amen.*

Let me conclude by sharing with you the words that overflowed my heart one Friday some years ago as I prepared to lead my own congregation in worship on Good Friday.

I have titled this "A Friday's Remembrance:"

This day I come to celebrate
The day You died to consecrate
    A race forlorn;
Which 'til You came,
Was without hope or champion.
You came, what incongruity.
    God is man.
Eternity's confined to time
That men might be
    Renewed to live in dignity.
To reconcile, a battle plan
    Is laid to purchase peace.
You spanned
The chasm carved by human sin.
Your cross quake closed the breach between.
That Friday has named this one "Good."
How can it be?
    We spilled Your blood.

What guilt.

Yet, good, I hear You say,

"My new creation birthed this day."

While birth pangs break Your body there,

On Calvary, my stripes You wear.

　Your wounded hands,

　　　　Your heart,

　　　　　　Your side,

Are flowing, Lord, a healing tide.

And so this day's remembrance

Remembering, remembering,

　The cost,

　　　　The cross,

　　　　　　The Christ, God's Son.

Lord Jesus, it's to You I come.

I come to take, I come to drink

Again of grace,

And here I think

What great salvation you afford.

I've been redeemed,

　Returned,

　　　　Restored.

I live again because You died,

Partake the feast Your love provides.

　　　I break Your body,

　　　　　Take Your blood,

While seated at Your table, Lord.

This leper, clean.
This blind man sees.
Your cross, the doubly healing key.
Now freeing me from death's decay.
Now flooding life with endless day.
Amen. Amen.

Raised by hate upon a hill,
stark there stands a cross of wood.
Look, the man they take and
kill is the Lamb, the Son of God.
See the blood now freely flow.
   "It is finished!" hear Him cry.
Who can understand or know,
Death has won, yet death will die.
Slashing wounds now scar the Lamb,
Blemish free until He's slain.
Hammer blows into His hand
Thunder forth again, again.
See His body raised in scorn;
See the spear now split His side.
Yet the victory shall be won
   By this man,
      Thus crucified.
Look, the cross now raised on high
Symbol of Christ's reign above.

Cowering demons fear and fly

Driven before the flame of love.

All of hell is mystified;

Satan thought this hour his gain.

See God's wisdom glorified,

Death destroyed,

In Jesus name.

  All is well, all is well,

Through Calvary's triumph

  All is well, all is well, all is well.

Through Christ, our conquerer,

  All is well, all is well, all is well.

In Jesus name,

  Now all is well.